FEARLESS:

FACING THE FUTURE CONFIDENTLY WITH RELATIONAL ESTATE PLANNING

JOSHUA E. HUMMER, ESQ.

ANNA MICHAL

Cover design: Anna Curtis // somethingsofresh.com

Interior design: Emily Borstad

First printing 2020

Printed in the United States of America

Trade Paperback ISBN: 978-1-7345538-0-2

Unless otherwise indicated, Scripture quotations are from the ESV Bible (The Holy Bible, English Standard Version), copyright 2001 by Crossway, a publishing ministry of Good News Publishers. All rights reserved.

In order to protect the identity of our clients, the names and details of stories in this book have been drastically changed or invented to protect the individuals involved.

A WORD OF THANKS

We would like to thank all our clients, whose stories have time and again shown us the great importance of relational estate planning. We value each and every opportunity to serve you and your families.

We're also grateful to Carley Walker and Steve Maclin, who sparked the idea of a book in our minds, and to Susan Dreyer and Larry Marsh, for taking time to proofread our first manuscripts and give us much needed feedback.

Lastly, to our friends Emily Borstad, Steven Reid, and the entire Relational Law team, thank you. We couldn't have done this without you.

CONTENTS

INTRODUCTION

I have been an estate planning attorney for over 12 years. Estate planning is just a fancy legal term for planning what happens to your assets (your "estate") after you die. For most of those 12 years, I did exactly what your average estate planning lawyer does: I drafted wills, trusts, powers of attorney, and more. I advised clients about how to maximize income, minimize taxes, protect their assets, and reduce risks. It all made sense on paper. But as the years passed, I began to feel I was missing something.

I noticed it most when I saw my clients struggle with emotional pain due to difficult relationships or their own approaching death. What did I have to offer someone who was dying? Tax savings? It felt as empty as it sounds. What solution could I give to someone who was estranged from a child or a parent? A well-written trust? It did not even begin to address the real issues.

As my misgivings grew, I finally pinpointed the source of that nagging feeling. I realized that although the services I provided were necessary, they fell short of what people needed. When someone is dying, losing a loved one, or dealing with a difficult family member, money is not the most important thing-relationships are.

I started pondering what, if anything, I could do to help people who found themselves wading through grief, loss, fear, and regret. My team and I started asking ourselves: can estate planning go farther than money? Can it help people with their relationships? And if so, how?

What we found changed my life and my practice. We discovered that estate planning provides a unique and powerful opportunity to impact relationships, pass on values and beliefs, and highlight meaning and purpose in a person's life.

Estate planning forces people to look at death, and nothing puts the important matters of life in perspective like death does. We began encouraging clients to start estate planning by thinking about their relationships, starting with their family and close friends and extending to the larger community they were involved in. We assured them we would get to money issues later, but told them that first, they should to ask themselves what they were afraid of, who they were worried for, and what they wanted others to remember about them. After we explored and established their goals, we moved on to figuring out how money could help accomplish those goals.

We also started introducing clients to new estate planning tools, such as ethical wills, the gifts and memories list, and estate guides and inventories. While none of these are as common as wills and trusts, they each allow clients to achieve their relational goals in different, non-monetary ways. Armed with both the traditional tools, such as wills and trusts, and these new tools, clients were able to craft relational estate plans that addressed the most important things in their lives - whether it was a damaged relationship, a struggling child, or a cherished cause.

The results were incredible. We watched as our clients considered possibilities for end-of-life planning they had never imagined. They started thinking bigger. They got excited. But most importantly, as they completed plans that were focused on their relationships, their fears were replaced by peace of mind and confidence about the future.

It was a powerful moment when someone put their last signature on their relational estate plan. Almost every client would sit back, breathe deeply, and say something like, "I'm so glad I finally did this." I could sense the relief as they realized that the most important things would live on after they were gone. They had truly done all they could for their family, friends, and community.

It was seeing the relief and confidence in our clients that motivated Anna and me to write this book. As the chaos, turmoil, and pain of our world continues to grow, we want to help as many people as possible experience the peace of mind that relational estate planning offers. We want everyone to become Fearless!

But I won't lie to you. Relational estate planning is harder and more difficult than traditional estate planning. It requires more work and forethought because relationships are more complicated than money. Normally, estate planning focuses on three things:

- who gets your assets when you pass
- who gets to control the collection and distribution of your assets
- how you can increase the amount of assets you leave

But in relational estate planning, you focus on how you can use your assets to benefit your family, friends, and community.

Traditional Estate Planning	Relational Estate Planning
Focuses on your assets	Focuses on your relationships
Asks who gets your assets	Asks how your assets are used
Limits your legacy to your finances	Expands your legacy to your values and beliefs
Does not include your life history and experiences	Preserves your history and experiences for others

Fearless is designed to help you explore relational estate planning and think about how it could work for you and your loved ones. Anna and I have laid out the book in three sections:

Section One goes through the five goals of a relational estate plan. We believe that a holistic relational estate plan incorporates elements from each of these goals, but we realize that for your specific situation, some may be a higher priority than others. For each goal, we explain why we believe it is important, and tell you the characteristics of a plan that will accomplish that goal. By the end of Section One, you'll be able to form a vision for how you can use relational estate planning for your family, friends, and community.

Section Two describes eight tools that you can use to implement a relational estate plan. We dive into the details of each tool, its purpose, and how it fits into relational estate planning. We will also give you some practical tips for how to use each one. At the end of Section Two, you will understand the tools that can help you accomplish the goal for your relational estate plan.

Section Three will help you start creating your relational estate plan. It contains a chapter on the next steps, along with several resources to help you as you walk through the process.

Our hope and prayer is that you will create a relational estate plan and discover how freeing it is to become Fearless as you face whatever the future holds.

Looking forward to your journey,

Josh

INTRODUCTION

_____

THE FIVE GOALS OF RELATIOAL ESTATE PLANNING

_____

"'EVERYONE KNOWS THEY'RE GOING TO DIE' HE SAID AGAIN, 'BUT NOBODY BELIEVES IT. IF WE DID, WE WOULD DO THINGS DIFFERENTLY.'"
-Mitch Albom, Tuesdays with Morrie

You can't create a plan until you know what you want it to do. That's why the first step to you becoming fearless is understanding the goals of relational estate planning and what your plan should accomplish.

For now, don't get caught up in the details of what kind of documents need to be drawn up or whether you need a will or a trust. We'll get to that, but those details are just tools that allow you to accomplish your vision. If you don't take the time to think through what your plan should do, the best tools in the world won't be able to help you.

Remember, relationships, not money, are the foundation of a relational estate plan. So, to determine what your relational estate plan should do, let's start with the people you love.

GOAL 1: PROTECT AND PROVIDE FOR LOVED ONES

The number one aim of a relational estate plan is to protect and provide for loved ones. This is much more than just tossing money at someone and hoping their problems will go away. It means meeting their financial, functional, and emotional needs.

GOAL 2: AVOID CONFLICT

Relational estate plans also avoid conflict. Unfortunately, a huge percentage of families struggle with conflict after the passing of a loved one, and disputes about money strain even the closest relationships. A relational estate plan creates harmony, not division, and invites people to come together after you're gone.

GOAL 3: LEAVE A LEGACY

You've lived, learned, felt, and done. What did you learn that can help others? What causes, ideas, or principles were important to you? What do you want to leave behind? This is your legacy, and a relational estate plan should communicate that legacy to your family, friends, and community.

GOAL 4: PRESERVE SPECIAL MEMORIES

Life is made up of shared memories. A relational estate plan should preserve those memories for your loved ones. When you take steps to preserve your memories with others, you do more than help them remember. You comfort them while they are grieving, and you give them a tangible piece of who you are to carry with them.

GOAL 5: EASE BURDENS

Last, but certainly not least, your relational estate plan should ease burdens. Your death will be a complicated and challenging time for your close family and friends. Some of those challenges will be practical and others emotional, but there are steps you can take ahead of time to make their burdens easier to bear.

In the next five chapters, we will walk through why each goal is important on your journey to becoming fearless, and what a plan that accomplishes each goal looks like. Let's start with the primary goal: protecting and providing for your loved ones.

CHAPTER 1:

GOAL 1: A RELATIONAL ESTATE PLAN

PROTECTS AND PROVIDES

FOR YOUR LOVED ONES

"THE GREAT USE OF LIFE IS TO SPEND IT FOR SOMETHING THAT WILL OUTLAST IT."

-William James

It's surprising to us how many people leave their families or close friends in a vulnerable position when they die. And it's not necessarily because they are lacking a trust or a will, although sometimes that is the case. More often, it's because they did not foresee and address obvious needs and their loved ones suffer because of it.

It could be that they haven't left enough funds to take care of family members or that they left their estates a confusing mess. Maybe they didn't do their taxes properly and left them to fall on their executor's shoulders. Perhaps they were hoarders, and now their family must wade through piles of personal posessions. Maybe they caused a rift in the family by publicly favoring one relative. There are countless ways a person's death can cause their family and friends to struggle.

Few of these people are uncaring or malicious. They love their families and want the best for them. But they do not grasp how they are going to affect the people around them when they die. As a result, they end up harming rather than helping their loved ones. This is why the first priority of a relational estate plan is to protect and provide for people-so that you don't accidentally hurt someone you love.

No two people, families, or life situations are the same, and there is no "one-size-fits-all, estate plan your way to a happy ending!" formula. You will have to think deliberately about what it means for you to protect and provide for your loved ones, and you will have to think a lot bigger than just money.

HOW TO PROTECT AND PROVIDE FOR YOUR LOVED ONES

If you want to protect and provide for your loved ones, you must create a plan that has five characteristics. We've listed them below and will explore each one:

- It is based on an analysis of true needs.
- It avoids the "money dump."
- It meets financial needs.
- It meets functional needs.
- It meets emotional needs.

CHARACTERISTIC 1: A PLAN THAT PROTECTS AND PROVIDES FOR LOVED ONES IS BASED ON AN ANALYSIS OF TRUE NEEDS.

How do you determine what your loved ones will need when you are gone? You start by asking three big questions: Who needs you? What do they need? Why do they need it? We call this a "true needs" analysis because it is designed to help you uncover the actual needs of your loved ones, rather than what their needs appear to be at first glance.

The first question to ask is, "Who needs you?" Consider your relationships for a moment. Who depends on you for some type of care or support? It's not just parents and spouses who need to think about this question. Chances are you play a crucial role in at least one other person's life.

It could be those who financially depend on you, such as minor children. But it could also be the elderly aunt you help with household repairs and lawn maintenance. It could be the friend who struggles emotionally and leans on you for support. It could be a sibling who looks to you for guidance about decisions. This is not a time to be modest but honest and objective. On a regular basis, we have clients who tells us that no one will miss them when they are gone. But in our experience, it's extremely rare for people to be completely independent of others.

Once you have a mental list of the people in your life who need you, ask yourself what they need. What do you provide for them that will be missing once you are gone? What problems do you foresee in their future? Your loved ones might need money, but often, they need so much more than that. They need guidance, emotional support, and community. What kind of practical and emotional support do you provide for your loved ones now that will be lost to them once you are gone?

For example, a father of minor children needs to make sure there is enough money to take care of them. But kids need more than just money. They need encouragement, advice, and love. So, in addition to leaving financial assets for his children, he could ask a few men he respects to look out for and guide his children if he is no longer there.

A woman with a disabled partner will want to make sure he has enough money to live on, but again, that's only a start. She needs to make sure he or his caretaker knows where the funds are and how they should be invested or used. She should also make sure that, when she is gone, someone will physically care for him and that there are people in his life to emotionally support him. These are all "what" he needs.

This part of estate planning requires you to take inventory of what will help your loved ones face the future. You must observe where they are in life and understand how you are involved with their journeys.

After you think about what your beneficiaries need, think about why they need what they need. Let's stick with the example of a father of minor children. The "why" is easy. They need money to survive because they aren't old enough to take care of themselves. However, what if the children have grown and they still need money because they've made poor decisions in life? Now, the children's need for money is really a manifestation of deeper issues-the need for wisdom, discipline, financial discretion, and maybe even psychological help. So ask yourself, "why do my loved ones have the needs they do? What are the root causes of those needs?" You can't "fix" someone you love, but are there ways that you can address what's really going on or at least not make their issues worse?

Again, these questions are rarely easy or quick to answer, but you cannot expect to protect and provide for people if you don't understand what they truly need.

CHARACTERISTIC 2: A PLAN THAT PROTECTS AND PROVIDES FOR LOVED ONES AVOIDS THE "MONEY DUMP."

Outside of basic survival demands, money is very rarely the real solution to someone's problems. And even when it is part of the solution, it's usually not the most important part. But many people who create an estate plan focus exclusively on their money and on leaving it to whomever they feel the closest. They end up dropping money into the laps of family members or friends, without any consideration for their true needs or how the money will impact them. We've dubbed this common practice the "money dump."

Leaving money to loved ones is not bad. Sometimes it is exactly what a person needs. However, leaving money to a loved one without thinking about how it will impact them can end up hurting, not helping them.

Over the years, I (Josh) have watched many, many families find out the hard way that:

- People who have made bad choices will continue to make those same choices after receiving an inheritance that was supposed to help them.
- What was meant to be a meaningful monetary gift is often spent in a way the giver would never have wanted.
- Money doesn't address deeper emotional needs and does not fix damaged relationships.

A relational estate plan takes into consideration that direct access to money is not always the answer to a person's true needs and avoids the money dump.

CHARACTERISTIC 3: A PLAN THAT PROTECTS AND PROVIDES FOR LOVED ONES MEETS FINANCIAL NEEDS.

Now that we have discussed the wrong way to meet financial needs, let's discuss how they should be met-with the right amount of money, the right amount of control, and the right amount of direction.

THE RIGHT AMOUNT OF MONEY

How much money should you leave a loved one? To answer this question, you need to understand both their current financial state and the impact your gift may have on them. How much to leave depends on their age, their location, their earning potential, and other resources available to them. You also need to consider the rising cost of living and unforeseen expenses they might have. As you evaluate all these factors, remember that money sometimes changes how people behave. You must consider what temptations come along with large sums of money.

I (Josh) once knew a young man whose aunt died suddenly. He knew he was her heir, but he did not know how much money he would be inheriting. Since he was from out of state and in a bad financial position, he had difficulty paying for a flight to come and get his inheritance. However, after he arrived and found out he was inheriting over one million, he showed up to my office in a brand-new Corvette, without giving any thought to how he would get it home. Money can tempt people to make rash decisions.

Short of a crystal ball, there's no way to determine the exact amount you'll need to ensure a smooth financial future for your loved one. However, if you consider what someone will need and how the gift will impact them, you will be in the best possible position to make an educated guess.

Before we move on, we want to point out a common problem people encounter when thinking through this issue. What do you do when someone needs more than you can give them? If you are in this situation, you need to consider how your loved one can make up the difference. Does your spouse or child have the skills or education to get a job if need be? Will they need to move to a different home? Is there some way you can set them up now to provide them with more when you are gone? It's like the old adage says, "Give a man a fish, and you feed him for a day. Teach a man to fish, and you feed him for a lifetime."

THE RIGHT AMOUNT OF CONTROL

Once you determine the amount of money you think someone

needs, you'll have to decide how much control they should have over it. You can use your estate plan to set limits on how and when money you leave can be used.

Some people have the discipline and financial sense to safely receive a monetary gift. But what if a loved one with a financial need has difficulty handling money well? Many people have family members they love dearly, but who struggle with drugs, gambling, or spending issues. Giving family members like these control over an inheritance will most likely intensify their harmful life choices. In these instances, you should limit the amount of control someone has over the money you leave to protect and provide for them.

Beth gave us a great example of how to use control to meet financial needs. She had two adult sons, Phil and Gerald. Phil was bi-polar and struggled with depression and suicidal tendencies. As a result, Phil had never been able to keep a job and lived on welfare. Gerald was a successful dentist with a wife and three young children. When Beth was putting her estate plan together, she recognized that Phil had financial needs, but if she gave him money, he would just use it to harm himself as he had done before. When she died, instead of leaving a lump sum of money to Phil, she created a trust for him. The trust gave Phil a set amount of money each month for living expenses, and, if he needed more, he had to get approval from the local bank who managed the trust. This is a perfect example of someone meeting a financial need by not giving their loved one control over a gift.

You may be on the other side of the spectrum, where you need to guarantee that your beneficiary has control over their inheritance so that other family members cannot abuse it or steal from them. Either way, the issue of control is important and one you should consider carefully.

THE RIGHT AMOUNT OF DIRECTION

Finally, to meet a financial need, you must decide what directions or instructions your loved one needs to use your gift well. Far too frequently, we see people leave enough financial resources for loved ones but then fail to tell them how to use those resources well. Giving instructions does not mean you have to be overbearing or a micromanager. Sometimes it's as simple as telling your loved ones which bank you use. On the other hand, your instructions can be as complex as investment advice or diversification ratios. If your loved ones depend on you financially, they most likely do not know as much about managing money as you do. Many people find it difficult to handle finances well. So even if you trust a loved one not to waste funds, they may need directions on how to manage them.

It could also be that the best direction you can give is a list of professionals you trust. If you have relationships with a financial advisor, accountant, or attorney, make sure your loved ones know who they are and have their contact information in case they need help.

In summary, your directions should include where your assets are located, your thoughts on the best way to use them, and where your loved ones can and should go for help if they need it. If the people in your life have legitimate financial needs, it's not always easy to know how to provide for them. But if you follow these principles, you can avoid many of the most common mistakes people make and create a plan to meets your loved ones' financial needs.

CHARACTERISTIC 4: A PLAN THAT PROTECTS AND PROVIDES FOR LOVED ONES MEETS FUNCTIONAL NEEDS.

Functional needs are practical, everyday living needs. They can be as simple as whether your spouse knows how to use the lawn mower all the way to how to run a family business. In my family, I (Josh) handle the finances and taxes because my wife does not like to do them, and she handles the lawnmowing and yard care because of my allergies. If something happened to me, my wife would have to start handling the finances and taxes. And, if something happened to her, I would have to start doing the lawnmowing and yard care. These are examples of functional needs. If you are having trouble pinpointing your loved ones' needs, ask yourself these questions: Are there any household responsibilities that you alone know how to manage? What do you regularly do for your family or friends that no else knows how to do or is willing to do?

If functional needs aren't met, it can cause serious problems, as Bill's family found out. Bill was an accountant who never married and had no children. But he was very close to his nieces and nephews. One of the ways he stayed close to them was that he prepared and filed their income tax returns each year. He loved doing it because it gave him an excuse to see each one of them and talk to them throughout the year. However, when he died suddenly, his family members found themselves at a loss for how to do taxes. One of them was even audited by the IRS as a result. Bill failed to foresee and meet his family's functional need for someone else to do their income tax returns.

In contrast, Joseph's parents foresaw and met his functional needs. Joseph was 48, autistic, and non-verbal. He was a very sweet man, but with the mental capacity of a five-year old. For years, his parents took care of him financially and functionally. As they grew older, they started thinking about his needs, who he would live with, and who would watch over him when they were gone. Because of his dear relationship with his sister, Audrey, they asked her. She agreed, and they created an estate plan which not only met his financial needs but also provided housing and financial compensation for Audrey as she became Joseph's functional caretaker. This is a wonderful example of meeting functional needs well.

Functional needs can be met in two main ways. You can provide information, or you can provide relationships. Basic functional needs can be met by providing information that someone will need to take over what you do now. For example, you might leave directions on how to pay certain bills or maintain a piece of equipment. For more complicated functional needs, you should identify people with whom your loved one can form new relationships to meet those needs. Think about both Bill and Joseph. To meet his family's functional need for tax returns, Bill could have left them the contact information for another accountant or tax expert he trusted. This new relationship would have met their functional need to do their taxes. Joseph's parents did this. They identified a new caretaker relationship for Joseph, and they included it in their estate plan.

CHARACTERISTIC 5: A PLAN THAT PROTECTS AND PROVIDES FOR LOVED ONES MEETS EMOTIONAL NEEDS.

Emotional needs are the hardest needs to identify and meet. They vary greatly from person to person and from family to family. It would be overly ambitious and naive to think that your estate plan is the answer to someone else's unhealed pain or personal struggles. But a relational estate plan can fortify, strengthen, and contribute to the emotional well-being of your loved ones in three ways: by reminding loved ones of their relationship with you, by encouraging relationships with others, and by reminding them of your purpose and their involvement in it.

You may have told someone that you love or care for them many times in the past. But, if you include it in your estate plan, you can continue reminding them of it long after you're gone.

Your plan should also encourage relationships between your loved ones. To do this well, you must avoid conflict. This is critical to a relational estate plan and we will discuss how to accomplish this in the next chapter. But more than just avoiding conflict, your plan should strengthen relationships when you are gone. You can do this in several ways. It could look like anything from asking one person to check in on another to setting money aside to pay for annual family vacations.

Finally, you can use your plan to remind your family and friends of your purpose and their involvement in it. This is part of leaving a legacy, which is the third goal of relational estate planning. We will go into detail on how to do this in a later chapter.

PROTECTING AND PROVIDING FOR LOVED ONES: AN EXAMPLE

Before we conclude this chapter, we want to give you an illustration of how to protect and provide for someone. It's an example from Jesus, the author of the golden rule. Whether or not you are a Christian or religious isn't the point here–we can all learn something from Jesus's relational estate plan.

The Gospels record that as Jesus was dying on the cross, he made a tender statement to his mother and close friend, John:

> When Jesus saw his mother standing there beside the disciple he loved, he said to her, 'Dear woman, here is your son.' And he said to this disciple, 'Here is your mother.' And from then on this disciple took her into his home.
> -John 19:26-27, NLT.

In two short verses, we see Jesus, Mary, and John share an exchange that was a far cry from a sterile fiscal transaction. Even as Jesus was suffering terribly, he considered his mother and what she would need when he was gone. He recognized that she would have financial, emotional, and functional needs that he, as her first-born son, would no longer be able to meet. And so, he asked John to treat Mary as his own mother. Yes, Jesus was arranging financial provision for Mary, but he was also doing something much deeper. He was asking John to love and care for Mary as a son would his own mother. In doing so, Jesus captured the essence of what it meant to protect and provide for a loved one.

CHAPTER 1 SUMMARY

The first goal of a relational estate plan is to protect and provide for your loved ones. This means thinking deliberately about your loved ones and making sure you do not accidentally harm them. A plan that accomplishes this goal has these five characteristics:

- Characteristic 1: It is based on an analysis of true needs.

- Characteristic 2: It avoids the "money dump."

- Characteristic 3: It meets financial needs.

- Characteristic 4: It meets functional needs.

- Characteristic 5: It meets emotional needs.

CHAPTER 2:

_____

GOAL 2: A RELATIONAL ESTATE PLAN

AVOIDS CONFLICT

_____

"FAMILY QUARRELS ARE BITTER THINGS. THEY DON'T GO ACCORDING
TO ANY RULES. THEY'RE NOT LIKE ACHES OR WOUNDS, THEY'RE MORE
LIKE SPLITS IN THE SKIN THAT WON'T HEAL BECAUSE THERE'S NOT
ENOUGH MATERIAL."

-F. Scott Fitzgerald

Frank was an elderly widower who had a daughter and two sons. He was a kind man who lived alone for the last ten years of his life. His daughter lived nearby and helped him with everything from doctor appointments and grocery store runs to cooking meals and cleaning his old farmhouse. His two sons, however, rarely came to see him. One hadn't seen Frank in five years, and the other only saw him once a year at Christmas.

When Frank created his estate plan, it seemed only natural that his daughter should get the largest portion. After all, their relationship was obviously the closest, and she had sacrificed much to care for him. So, Frank allotted a few thousand dollars to each son, then he left the rest of his assets, several hundred thousand dollars, to his daughter. When Frank passed away, his sons found out about their father's decision. They were furious. They accused their sister of stealing from them, even though she'd had nothing to do with Frank's decision. To this day, both brothers refuse to speak to their sister, and they continue to slander her to other family members and friends.

We can't think of anyone we've ever worked with who wanted their loved ones to fight once they passed, but unfortunately, Frank's story is all too common. Death is sorrowful enough, but the ensuing arguments, hurt feelings, anger, and, at times, even lawsuits between loved ones makes it downright bitter.

No matter who you are and how confident you may be in the emotional bonds between your loved ones, you must go into estate planning with the understanding that money complicates things. Our clients often say things like "I know my kids. I know my spouse. There won't be a lawsuit in my family. That would never happen." Maybe they're right. Maybe their family wouldn't resort to suing each other over inheritance issues (although many, many families find themselves in that exact situation). But the tension, damaged friendships, and familial estrangement you can cause by not preparing well can be just as devastating. Your spouse may be level-headed and trustworthy. Your children may love each other and be mature. But no one is above misunderstandings, hurt feelings, or responding emotionally to perceived unfairness.

Because of the damage that this type of conflict can cause to relationships, the second goal of a relational estate plan is to avoid conflict. Each family is different and has its own dynamics, and sometimes conflict may seem inevitable. But, that shouldn't stop you from doing everything you can to ensure that your loved ones remain on good terms with each other after you're gone.

HOW TO AVOID CONFLICT

An estate plan that avoids conflict has these five characterisics:

- Characteristic 1: It contains clear directions.
- Characteristic 2: It treats loved ones equally whenever possible and appropriate.
- Characteristic 3: It uses trusted personal representatives.

- Characteristic 4: It explains decisions.
- Characteristic 5: It highlights the importance of relationships over money.

CHARACTERISTIC 1: A PLAN THAT AVOIDS CONFLICT CONTAINS CLEAR DIRECTIONS.

A relational estate plan must have clear instructions. We cannot emphasize this enough. When you are articulating instructions on what you want to happen when you are gone, do not be vague! If an estate plan can be interpreted in different ways by different people, it creates an opportunity for conflict. And though something may seem clear to you, it may not be clear in the legal world. Ultimately, your will and other legal documents are not written for you or to you. They are written for and to a judge. Yes, they are written about you and your estate, but if there are any problems or someone contests what is written, a judge will be the one to decide what your documents actually mean. This is one reason why you need legal help to create your relational estate plan. If you use an attorney who understands how judges interpret legal language, you can draft documents with clear instructions and avoid conflict over vague language.

CHARACTERISTIC 2: A PLAN THAT AVOIDS CONFLICT TREATS LOVED ONES EQUALLY.

If you favor one family member or friend over others, you are asking for conflict. This could mean giving one child more than the others or including a distant relative along with close relatives. Things get even more complicated for blended families. How do you divide your assets if you have biological children and stepchildren? What do you do if you have children with your current spouse as well as children from a previous marriage? What if your spouse is not the parent of your children? How you handle these scenarios will depend on your specific circumstances, but we recommend you use this general principle: When appropriate and possible, treat each of your biological children equally. If you do not have children, then try to treat your closest relatives equally. Whether or not you include stepchildren is up to you, but be consistent. For example, if one spouse leaves the other spouse's children out, then both spouses should. If you include one stepchild, you should include all stepchildren. In our experience, people who divide their estates equally end up causing significantly less conflict amongst their loved ones.

All that being said, we realize these guidelines won't work for every situation. Many people believe that one or several people in their life should receive more than the others. For these situations, your plan must explain clearly why more is being given to certain people. If you take time to explain your thinking, you can minimize people assuming the worst or jumping to inaccurate conclusions.

CHARACTERISTIC 3: A PLAN THAT AVOIDS CONFLICT USES TRUSTED PERSONAL REPRESENTATIVES.

When you create a relational estate plan, you will need to choose one or more people to implement that plan. Depending on the role they play and the state they are in, these people are called either executors, administrators, trustees, personal representatives, or agents. For our purposes, we will refer to all of them as personal representatives. If you want to avoid conflict, name personal representatives that are liked and trusted by your beneficiaries. In most estate plans, personal representatives have broad discretion, meaning they get to decide many of the details of how your assets are divided. If you pick someone who has a bad reputation, other family members may assume they are being treated unfairly, even if that's not true. If you pick someone who is incapable of dealing with disagreements wisely, small issues may grow into major conflicts. Carefully consider who in your life can best execute your wishes while simultaneously treating others fairly and keeping the peace.

CHARACTERISTIC 4: A PLAN THAT AVOIDS CONFLICT EXPLAINS DECISIONS.

We've mentioned it several times already, but it's important enough to say again: a relational estate plan must over-communicate the reasons why you made the decisions you did. Don't assume people will understand the reason you chose one person and not another to be your personal representative, or why you left one child a greater share, or why you left money to a charitable cause. You must tell them.

In addition to including explanations in your estate plan, we recommend you tell your beneficiaries about these decisions now, while you are around to answer questions and provide further explanations. Explaining yourself now ensures your family and friends understand why you've made the choices you have. If you keep your estate plan a secret because you're afraid someone will be unhappy about it, that's a sure sign that conflict is ahead. If you do tell your beneficiaries about your plan ahead of time, make sure you keep them informed about any changes. No one enjoys being blindsided by legal or financial surprises, particularly during a time of mourning.

CHARACTERISTIC 5: A PLAN THAT AVOIDS CONFLICT HIGHLIGHTS THE IMPORTANCE OF RELATIONSHIPS OVER MONEY.

The last and possibly the most important thing you can do to avoid conflict is to use your estate plan to communicate what your loved ones meant to you. To understand why this is important, you need to understand why conflict occurs over people's assets when they are gone. Sometimes people are just downright greedy, but most times, that is not the whole story. There are many genuine, kind people who end up arguing over family money. We've seen people who were normally levelheaded fight over assets so small they weren't even worth the legal fees it cost to make the arguments. Why did they do this? Because fights like these aren't really about money. They are about people's perceptions of their relationship with the person who died. People get upset more by what they think the money represents, their value to their deceased loved one, than the money itself. When someone such as Frank's sons receives less money than another relative, or they aren't made the personal representative, they tend to think they were loved less, valued less or worth less than others. And they can't accept that, so they fight it, even when the actual item or amount isn't worth fighting over.

To put it another way, conflicts over inheritances get ugly when people equate money with love, value, and worth. Such conflicts are hurtful and messy and they tear relationships apart during an already painful time. You can avoid this type of conflict by clearly telling people what they meant to you. Don't leave a family member or close friend wondering how you felt about them, don't assume your loved ones will automatically understand why you value them, and don't expect them to read your mind. Avoid conflict by expressing what they meant to you.

While there is no way to know this, I (Josh) firmly believe that if Frank had included just one or two of these characteristics in his plan, there is a good chance it would have avoided the nasty family split that occurred when he died. To avoid a similar outcome, make sure your plan contains the characteristics explained in this chapter.

Estate planning may conjure up visions of paperwork, figures, and signatures in your mind. And traditional estate planning does, in fact, focus a good deal on documents and money. But relational estate planning aims to promote peace before it focuses on money, because the unity of your loved ones is much more important than who gets your assets.

CHAPTER 2 SUMMARY

The second goal of your relational estate plan should be to avoid conflict. Conflict between loved ones over a deceased person's assets is frequent and vicious. Remember, money complicates things, and you should never assume your family and friends are above the potential for conflict.

To avoid conflict, your relational estate plan should have these five characteristics:

- Characteristic 1: It contains clear directions.

- Characteristic 2: It treats loved ones equally whenever appropriate and possible.

- Characteristic 3: It uses trusted personal representatives.

- Characteristic 4: It explains decisions.

- Characteristic 5: It highlights relationships over money.

CHAPTER 3:

_____

GOAL 3: A RELATIONAL ESTATE PLAN

LEAVES YOUR LEGACY

_____

"TELL ME, WHAT ELSE SHOULD I HAVE DONE?
DOESN'T EVERYTHING DIE AT LAST, AND TOO SOON?
TELL ME, WHAT IS IT YOU PLAN TO DO
WITH YOUR ONE WILD AND PRECIOUS LIFE?"

- Mary Oliver

No matter who you are, yours is a life worth remembering. Each of us lives and dies, fails and succeeds, cries and laughs, hurts and loves, but no one has done so the way you have. Maybe your life feels commonplace and unremarkable to you, but the truth is your story is unique. Anyone who has walked life's journey has a legacy to leave, and this legacy can have a tremendous impact on your family, friends, and community.

Our friend John loves the outdoors. He loves farms, fishing, and wildlife. Industrial developments and the urban sprawl are eyesores to him. He has spent much of his life outside, wonderstruck at nature's beauty. Several years ago, he and his wife decided that conservation would be their legacy. They donated a large portion of their many acres to conservation groups, and then he wrote an essay explaining his love for the outdoors and how he believes that heaven will be like his idyllic view of the Shenandoah Valley. You can read this beautiful essay on our website. He has already shared it with his church and his family and has asked that it be read at his funeral.

John's commitment to promoting conservation with his life and after his death is a wonderful example of a legacy. Legacies look very different from person to person, but we define a legacy this way: A person's legacy is the distinct mark of their life, which they both communicate and deliberately leave behind to affect other people, and it is always connected to something greater than themselves.

It is important to distinguish a legacy from good memories. Everyone leaves behind memories, but very few people leave a legacy. We've heard some incredible stories from clients over the years-stories of hope, perseverance, integrity, and sacrificial love. Before we discovered relational estate planning, we knew we were doing something important when we drew up clients' wills, set up their trusts, and notarized their documents. Yet, when the legal matters were wrapped up and we shook hands goodbye, we wondered whether anyone else would ever hear the stories of how the extraordinary artist created her best painting or how the Korean War veteran continued the fight for justice and freedom after his military days were over. They were just memories, destined to be forgotten. It saddens us that so many people live through the ups and downs of their lives, have incredible experiences, gain wisdom at the school of hard knocks, and then, they get to the end of their lives and just... die. They don't tell their world the things they learned; they don't ensure what they valued will be remembered.

This is why we believe so strongly in the importance of leaving a legacy and why it is a goal of relational estate planning. When you create a legacy, you do so much more than just share memories. You take what you have learned and create a plan to help others with those lessons when you are gone. A legacy blesses your family, friends, and community with the best parts of who you were. And it's not just something we have observed. Several scientific studies have proven that leaving a legacy has an incredible impact on both you and on those around you.

LEAVING A LEGACY IS GOOD FOR YOU

Several scientists have studied the impact of creating a legacy on terminally ill patients. They found that when these patients spend as little as thirty minutes thinking about their legacy their suffering and depression symptoms are significantly reduced. Another scientist studied these same patients and found that the process of creating a legacy reduced patients' distress about death, reinforced their sense of worth, and helped them attain a peaceful state. After reviewing all the research, Gene Cohen, the author of *The Mature Mind*, called creating a legacy "chocolate for the brain." Put simply, crafting your legacy is good for your mental health and well-being.

LEAVING A LEGACY IS GOOD FOR OTHERS

Beyond helping you, your legacy has the power to nourish, teach, and guide those around you. John Kunz, an expert in therapeutic reminiscences, has found that when someone leaves a legacy, it can benefit their loved ones in several important ways. It can:

- help them find meaning in life
- improve their problem-solving skills
- assist them in the grieving process
- increase the emotional support they need
- strengthen their self-esteem
- decrease their depression and anxiety

This is what a legacy can do for your family, friends, and community. Someday when your grandson doesn't think he's going to make it through med school, he'll need to remember how determination, responsibility, and resilience led you to work three jobs to provide for your family during times of financial hardship. Your legacy will inspire him to persevere. Someday when your niece is overwhelmed with grief over a miscarriage, she'll need to recall how your faith carried you through the devastating stillbirth of your child. Your spiritual legacy will give her hope in the storm of mourning.

Leaving a legacy isn't selfish. Rather, it's a gift. Honestly, failing to leave behind what you've learned is uncaring toward your loved ones and anyone else who may benefit. We are all affected by one another; our stories as people living the human experience are intertwined. John Donne wisely stated,

> No man is an island, entire of itself; every man is a piece of the continent, a part of the main. If a clod be washed away by the sea, Europe is the less, as well as if a promontory were, as well as if a manor of thy friend's or of thine own were: any man's death diminishes me, because I am involved in mankind, and therefore never send to know for whom the bells tolls; it tolls for thee.

-Devotions upon Emergent Occasions

IDENTIFYING YOUR LEGACY

If you want to leave a legacy, it might take you some time to figure out what you want your legacy to be. This isn't always easy, but it is more than worth the effort.

A legacy doesn't need to be "big." You may not have won the Nobel Peace Prize, but you've still done worthwhile things that should be shared. Maybe you promoted shopping locally in your community. Maybe you supported a certain right or political position. Maybe you raised your grandchildren in place of their struggling or absent parents. Each of these could be part of a legacy.

As you think through what your legacy should be, look for the big ideas, causes, and principles that mark your life. Any or all of these can be part of your legacy. If you still need help, we have a free guide and worksheet on our website that is designed to help you through the process. You can find a link to it in the resources section of this book.

HOW TO LEAVE A LEGACY

An estate plan that leaves a legacy should have these characteristics:

- Characteristic 1: It expressly states the legacy.
- Characteristic 2: It financially supports the legacy.
- Characteristic 3: It encourages others to remember the legacy.

CHARACTERISTIC 1: A PLAN THAT LEAVES A LEGACY EXPRESSLY STATES THE LEGACY.

Once you've pinpointed the causes, ideas, and values that are important to you, your estate plan should communicate them. Do not assume that your family, friends, and community will know or remember what was important to you. Tell them, and then tell them again. Your plan should make sure that your legacy is repeatedly communicated after you are gone. We will provide you with the tools to do this in Section Two.

CHARACTERISTIC 2: A PLAN THAT LEAVES A LEGACY FINANCIALLY SUPPORTS THE LEGACY.

This is the epitome of "put your money where your mouth is." One great way to show how important something was to you is to set aside money to support that cause or idea. For instance, let's say you want to leave a legacy related to education; you could leave money to a scholarship program at a school that impacted you. If your legacy is a passion for families, you could leave funds to be used for local parks or community centers. If your faith was important to you, you could donate to your local church or religious group. Whatever you decide, when you give to a charity, you leave an example for your loved ones and make a powerful statement about what you believed.

CHARACTERISTIC 3: A PLAN THAT LEAVES A LEGACY ENCOURAGES OTHERS TO REMEMBER THE LEGACY.

Lastly, your estate plan should encourage your community to keep remembering your legacy. There are many ways to do this, but here are a few ideas:

- Request that people donate money to an organization that supports a cause related to your legacy.

- Ask your family and close friends to read something about your legacy on your birthday

- Leave money to pay for your loved ones to do an activity related to your legacy.

We've seen many different approaches, but we'll end by telling you one of our favorites.

LEAVING A LEGACY: AN EXAMPLE

We once knew an elderly couple, Tim and Jane, who deeply valued family relationships. As they planned their estate, they realized that none of their children needed their money. Their children were well into adulthood and financially secure. So, Tim and Jane started thinking about what else they could do with their funds. It was important to them that their children and grandchildren remain connected to one another after their deaths. They considered several options and selected one we now call the vacation trust. When they died, Tim and Jane did not leave any money to their children or other family members. Instead, it all went into a trust. Each year after that, the trust paid for their children, grandchildren, and great-grandchildren to take a vacation together. If you ask the children (and we have), they will tell you how much they love this vacation and how close they are as a family because of it. Each year, the children talk frequently about where they want to go. The grandchildren have stayed close to their aunts, uncles, and cousins because of the annual vacation. And now, even the great-grandchildren are growing up with strong family relationships because of Tim and Jane's plan. It's a fantastic example of how you can use your estate plan to leave a legacy and remind those around you about what was important to you.

Your legacy is a priceless and immortal gift to your family, friends, and community. By creating a relational estate plan, you can ensure they enjoy this gift long after you're gone.

CHAPTER 3 SUMMARY

The third goal of a relational estate plan is to leave a legacy of what you learned and what you thought was important during your life. Leaving a legacy will not only benefit you, but it also will benefit your loved ones long after you are gone.

A plan that leaves a legacy has these three characteristics:

- Characteristic 1: It expressly states your legacy.

- Characteristic 2: It financially supports your legacy.

- Characteristic 3: It encourages others to remember your legacy.

CHAPTER 4:

GOAL 4: A RELATIONAL ESTATE PLAN

PRESERVES SPECIAL MEMORIES

"WE DON'T THINK OUR FATHERS WILL REALLY DIE, DO WE? THE ONES WHO SPEAK LOVE INTO OUR LIVES HAVE AN ETERNAL WAY ABOUT THEM."

-Donald Miller, "Scary Close"

It has been said many times that you don't ever truly get over the loss of someone you love. Grief, once experienced, can never really be erased from the human heart.

This was certainly true for our friend Elisabeth. We first met her when she and her husband came to us to help them craft their estate plan. She was vibrant, happy, and full of laughter. Several years later, she contacted us to let us know that her husband had passed. When we met with her the second time, she still smiled and even laughed a few times, but everything about her seemed solemn and weary. Grief had changed her. That's what grief does.

After author and public speaker Anne Lamott lost her father in her early 20s, and then her lifelong best friend in her 30s, she said this:

> You will lose someone you can't live without, and your heart will be badly broken, and the bad news is that you never completely get over the loss of your beloved. But this is also the good news. They live

forever in your broken heart that doesn't seal back up. And you come through. It's like having a broken leg that never heals perfectly—that still hurts when the weather gets cold, but you learn to dance with the limp.

Psychologists tell us that grief changes people. You may be familiar with the theory that there are five stages of grief. According to American-Swiss psychologist Elisabeth Kübler-Ross in her 1969 book, *On Death and Dying*, people who've experienced a major loss go through denial, arguing, bargaining, depression, (not necessarily in that order) and finally arrive at acceptance. The best-case scenario for someone in mourning is that they will grieve well and experience the first four stages as deeply as they need to, so that they can eventually move to the final stage of acceptance. But even after having reached this last stage, a person will be forever altered and in some state of grief for the rest of their life. Kübler-Ross said it this way:

> The reality is that you will grieve forever. You will not 'get over' the loss of a loved one; you will learn to live with it. You will heal, and you will rebuild yourself around the loss you have suffered. You will be whole again, but you will never be the same. Nor should you be the same, nor would you want to.

The people closest to you will inevitably enter their own journey of grief when you pass away. They will mourn their loss of you. It's not arrogant to think about this. It's just acknowledging the way things are. You've been a significant figure to certain people, and they will have to grapple with the reality that your role in their lives has ended.

The ways in which your family members and close friends will walk through the stages of grief over your death will be as individual as they are. One lady we know visited her husband's grave three times a day to talk to him for almost two years after his death. Another daughter is prone to frequent uncontrollable sobbing. A mother has a tattoo of her son's name on her arm.

Everyone processes grief differently, but one thing is for sure–everyone must go through it, and it is not easy. But though grief is extremely difficult, it's also healthy. The only way out is through, as they say. The best thing for a grieving loved one is to be able to grieve properly, instead of suppressing the hurt or trying to forget the deceased. While you won't be able to physically help your loved ones as they deal with your death, you can help them emotionally in the grieving process.

The fourth goal of a relational estate plan is to preserve memories. Preserving memories is related to but not the same as leaving your legacy. While leaving a legacy is focused on you and who you were, preserving memories is focused on others and what they meant to you. To understand why preserving memories will help your loved ones to grieve well, you need to understand the power of memories.

THE POWER OF SPECIAL MEMORIES

Think about how you are affected by memories of someone you've lost. In the immediate aftermath of losing someone, these memories can seem overwhelmingly painful. But as time passes, they become a comfort and an emotional connection to the deceased.

I've (Anna) experienced this since my grandmother died. She was beautiful and elegant, with a million-dollar smile and a laugh to match it. As I was growing up, she kept a painting by Andrew Wyeth hung in her room that mesmerized me. It pictures an old, cream-colored dog, curled up asleep on a four-poster bed with a white-tasseled blanket. Outside the window, a pine branch hovers, and light filters through to create a sunspot on the bed.

I used to lounge on her bed and study it, lost in its nostalgic simplicity. Years later, when it became clear that she was dying from cancer, she wanted me to have it. She's gone now; the painting hangs over my bed instead of hers. It reminds me of who she was and of our precious days together. Of course, I feel grief when I look at it sometimes. Of course, it makes me ache for her. Of course, I wish I could relive, even for a moment, the feeling of her quilt beneath me, the brightness of her bedroom, and the sound of her talking to me from the kitchen as I stared at the picture, hanging there on the wall like a sort of monument to childhood. But I also treasure it. Gazing at it might be bittersweet, but it also helps me process my emotions of heartache and emotionally reconnects me to a woman who deeply loved me. It opens the door in my mind to a hundred other memories of her that I never want to forget. That kind of pain is healing in some mysterious way.

In the days, months, and years following your death, your loved ones will want to remember the special moments they shared with you. They'll long to feel some type of connection to you, because they won't be able to physically connect with you any longer. By preserving memories for them, you will help them grieve well.

Scientists have confirmed that remembering positive experiences affects us in powerful ways. It lowers cortisol levels (a hormone associated with stress and mood swings) and activates areas of the brain connected to emotion regulation and mental strength. They've also found that happy memories will often interrupt the cascade of negative thoughts associated with depression. In other words, when someone dwells on a good memory, they can more easily gain a sense of calm and peace amid deep heartache. These memories won't make the pain of loss go away, but they will provide relief and joy despite it. We've seen it many times with families who have just lost a loved one. Grief hangs heavy in the air until someone remembers a story about the person who passed. "Wouldn't Dad have loved this?" "Do you remember when she did that?" And suddenly, piercing through the gloom, comes a memory. Smiles replace frowns, and laughter bursts out through tears. Preserving memories with your estate plan gives you the opportunity to create more moments like these for the people you love.

HOW TO PRESERVE MEMORIES

To accomplish the fourth goal of relational estate planning, preserving memories, your estate plan should have these three characteristics:

- Characteristic 1: It leaves meaningful items to specific people.
- Characteristic 2: It includes stories of shared memories.
- Characteristic 3: It encourages loved ones to re-experience memories.

CHARACTERISTIC 1: A PLAN THAT PRESERVES MEMORIES LEAVES MEANINGFUL ITEMS TO SPECIFIC PEOPLE.

Physical items are a great way to remind someone of a positive memory, just as the painting from Anna's grandmother does for her. It could be a memento from a trip you took together, or a picture of the two of you, or something of yours you know they'll treasure. By leaving someone personal property that is tied to a good memory, you are giving them a constant reminder of that memory.

CHARACTERISTIC 2: A PLAN THAT PRESERVES MEMORIES INCLUDES STORIES OF SHARED MEMORIES

In addition to leaving specific items, your estate plan should tell stories—stories of good times, shared difficulties, or even important milestones. In addition to reciting these stories, a relational estate plan should include a method of delivering these stories. Is there a story you want told at your funeral? How about one you want read every year on your birthday? It's also a great idea to pair physical items with stories. This enhances both; the story explains the physical item, and the physical items remind someone of the story.

CHARACTERISTIC 3: A PLAN THAT PRESERVES MEMORIES ENCOURAGES LOVED ONES TO RE-EXPERIENCE MEMORIES.

Lastly, your estate plan can encourage people to go back and re-experience places or activities they once shared with you. Try sending a loved one back to a certain place to giving them the tools they need to continue pursuing a hobby you enjoyed together. We know of one older gentleman who told his wife before he died, "Don't forget our flowers!" It was his way of reminding her of the peaceful hours they spent working in their garden together. And now, as she faithfully tends the garden, she remembers.

A relational estate plan that preserves memories will offer joy and comfort to your family and friends in the midst of their pain over losing you. It will help them learn to "dance with the limp."

CHAPTER 4: SUMMARY

The fourth goal of a relational estate plan is to preserve memories for your loved ones. Memories have tremendous power to provide joy and comfort during grief, and by preserving memories for your family and friends, your estate plan can help them grieve well when you are gone.

To preserve memories, a relational estate plan should have these three characteristics:

- Characteristic 1: It leaves meaningful items to specific people.

- Characteristic 2: It tells stories of shared memories.

- Characteristic 3: It encourages loved ones to re-experience memories.

CHAPTER 5:

GOAL 5: A RELATIONAL ESTATE PLAN

EASES BURDENS

RELATED TO YOUR PASSING

"BY SEIZING EVERY OPPORTUNITY FOR KINDNESS, FORGIVENESS, HEALING, AND LOVE THAT CROSSES MY PATH EACH DAY, I HOPE THAT MY DEATH, ALTHOUGH PERHAPS SAD FOR SOME, WILL BE GRACEFULLY CONCLUDED."

-Lisa J. Shultz, A Chance to Say Goodbye: Reflections on Losing a Parent

When Jack lost his beloved wife to a sudden heart attack, he didn't get the opportunity to quietly grieve. He had a hundred different loose ends to tie up. He had to deal with funeral directors. He had to pay bills. He had to make gravesite arrangements. He had to talk to family members and make travel and lodging arrangements. He had to figure out what to do with her many possessions. He told us bitterly, "I never knew how hard it was for a person to die." Her death happened in a moment, but its aftermath left him grappling with painful details for months.

The fact of the matter is, we're all going to die at some point. It's useless to pretend it won't happen. And when it does, it will be a difficult time for those you leave behind.

Louise and Elisabeth saw this first-hand when their sister, Margaret, died. Margaret was very healthy for her age, but died suddenly, at age 90. She had known she needed to redo her estate plan but didn't because, according to her, she was going to live quite a while longer. She wanted to leave most of her assets to charity, but her will was handwritten, hard to read, and vague. Her house was full of junk (she was a hoarder), and her finances were unorganized and spread among many different financial institutions. Louise and Elisabeth spent the next two years sorting through the details of Margaret's life and trying to get her assets organized to the point where they could finally be given to the charity she'd selected. Instead of being able to celebrate their sister and her decision to leave a legacy through charitable giving, Louise and Elisabeth spent two years frustrated and annoyed.

If you, like Margaret, leave people with a chaotic situation when you pass, the rest of your plan will lose much of its impact. The fifth and final goal of a relational estate plan is to ease the burdens on your loved ones from your passing. At first glance, this goal of relational estate planning may seem very similar to traditional estate planning, which frequently focuses on making things easier. But it is actually very different. Traditional estate planning focuses only on legal difficulties, not practical ones. Even then, easing burdens is usually less important than saving money. In a relational estate plan, the focus is on easing both legal and practical burdens as a primary goal.

HOW TO EASE BURDENS

A plan that eases burdens has these five characteristics:

- Characteristic 1: It is connected to a simplified life.
- Characteristic 2: It involves organized assets.
- Characteristic 3: It contains post-death instructions.
- Characteristic 4: It is updated regularly.
- Characteristic 5: It is designed to handle probate efficiently.

CHARACTERISTIC 1: A PLAN THAT EASES BURDENS IS CONNECTED TO A SIMPLIFIED LIFE.

The first characteristic of a plan that eases burdens really doesn't have anything to do with the plan itself. It has to do with your life. The simpler your life is, the less of a burden it will be for your loved ones to handle. So, simplify your life. Throw away or donate the things you don't use and that no one else will want. We aren't telling you to throw out important possessions or meaningful heirlooms. But most of us end up filling our homes with things we don't really need and that are not intimately connected to us. Do your loved ones a favor-go through your possessions on a regular basis and get rid of things.

For the past several years, my (Josh) family has taken a month-long summer vacation. Because we have a large family (four kids and two adults), we have to pack light. We pack five sets of clothes for each person. We also bring a small bag of toys and a small bag of books, plus some kitchen supplies. At first, we were worried that the kids would complain about having to wear the same clothes or not having a certain toy. But each year, nobody has said a word about not having enough stuff. We make do with what we have, and we have a lovely time. It has been eye-opening for my wife and me to realize that we don't need most of what we own. If you can easily live without something and don't use it often, consider getting rid of it.

CHARACTERISTIC 2: A PLAN THAT EASES BURDENS INVOLVES ORGANIZED ASSETS.

Dealing with a disorganized life is not the only thing that can cause burdens. Managing disorganized assets can be just as difficult. Your loved ones need to be able to find and access key information quickly. This is another characteristic of a relational estate plan that has more to do with your life than with the plan itself. To ease burdens for those you love, your life should be organized.

CHARACTERISTIC 3: A PLAN THAT EASES BURDENS CONTAINS POST-DEATH INSTRUCTIONS.

This next step might seem obvious, but to ease burdens for your family, your plan should have detailed instructions for when you are gone. This requires that you not only have a 30,000-foot view of the relational goals you want to accomplish, but also that you have a plan for the details of exactly how your assets will accomplish those goals. How is your retirement account going to protect your spouse? How will your brother get your car? What bills must be paid? What do you want for your funeral and burial? If you do not take the time to set out detailed instructions about all these things, someone else will have to bear that burden.

CHARACTERISTIC 4: A PLAN THAT EASES BURDENS IS UPDATED REGULARLY.

The next characteristic of a plan that eases burdens is that it is updated regularly. Several times a year, we meet with the loved ones of someone who has passed, and they tell us that the person who died was planning to update their estate plan, but they never got around to it. In almost every case, the loved ones had a much more difficult time than they would have if the person who died kept their plan up to date. For people with complicated estate plans, we recommend that they review and update their plans at least once a year. For simple plans, every two years may be enough. Either way, scheduling regular estate plan updates is vital.

CHARACTERISTIC 5: A PLAN THAT EASES BURDENS IS DESIGNED TO HANDLE PROBATE EFFICIENTLY.

Probate is seen as something to be avoided in the estate planning world. If you're familiar with it, you might have heard horror stories about how complicated and wearisome it can be. And some of those stories are true, but we've found that probate is a bit misunderstood.

Probate is the process a court uses to divide your assets when you die. If you make a last will and testament, the court ensures it is followed. If you don't make a will, the court will use default rules (called the intestacy rules) to determine who gets your stuff. Of course, the judge does not do this personally. They appoint a person (called a personal representative, executor, or administrator) to collect your assets, pay bills, and then distribute the assets. In most states, the judge also appoints an independent attorney or auditor to review and approve what the personal representative has done. This process varies from state to state, and in most states, the personal representative can take different paths depending on the size and complexity of the estate. In Virginia, one path through probate is as simple as filling out a one-page form, while another path could require hundreds of pages of legal filings and take years to complete.

As a result of how complicated probate can be, many people create estate plans that try to avoid probate. We will get into the details later, but there are ways you can pass your assets that do not involve going through probate. However, these plans to avoid probate are always more complicated to set up and maintain than other plans that use probate. In other words, if you want to ease burdens for your loved ones and avoid probate, you are going to have to spend more time, money, and energy on your estate plan now.

What is best for you and your loved ones will depend on your specific circumstances. For now, don't worry about exactly how your plan will handle probate. Instead, you simply need to understand that to ease burdens, a relational estate plan should be designed to handle probate efficiently. This could mean the plan avoids probate entirely, qualifies for one of the simpler ways through probate, or even anticipates hiring an attorney to handle the entire probate process. The important thing is not which option you choose but that your plan is designed to handle probate in a way that makes things easier on your loved ones.

CHAPTER 5 SUMMARY

The fifth goal of a relational estate plan is to ease burdens related to your passing. Easing burdens for your loved ones will allow them the space to grieve and the freedom to appreciate the rest of your relational estate plan.

To ease burdens, a relational estate plan should have these five characteristics:

- Characteristic 1: It is connected to a simplified life.

- Characteristic 2: It involves organized assets.

- Characteristic 3: It contains post-death instructions.

- Characteristic 4: It is updated regularly.

- Characteristic 5: It is designed to handle probate efficiently.

SECTION ONE SUMMARY

Let's recap. The first thing you need to do when you create your relational estate plan is identify what you want the plan to do. While your plan's details will be specific to you, it should have these five goals:

- Goal 1: Protect and Provide for your Loved Ones

- Goal 2: Avoid Conflict

- Goal 3: Leave a Legacy

- Goal 4: Preserve Memories

- Goal 5: Ease Burdens

For each goal, we've discussed why it is important and given you characteristics of a plan that accomplishes that goal. In this next section, we will turn from what a relational estate plan should do to the tools you can use to implement it.

RELATIONAL ESTATE PLANNING TOOLS

"I DON'T BELIEVE IN LUCK, I BELIEVE IN PREPARATION."

-Bobby Knight

Now that we have covered the goals that a relational estate plan should accomplish, let's talk about the tools you can use to accomplish those goals. Each of the following tools can be used in a relational estate plan. However, not everyone will use them all. Your relational estate plan should be tailored to you and your loved ones, and it should include the tools that are necessary to accomplish the goals of relational estate planning in your situation. As we explore each tool, we will go over what it is and how you can use it as part of your plan.

The first three tools are ones that everyone should include in their relational estate plan. These are: last wills and testaments, ethical wills, and estate guides and inventories. The last five tools are optional and will be useful to some people but not others. These are: trusts, beneficiary designations, gifts and memories lists, planned giving, and funeral arrangements and directives. Before we dive into the weeds, here is a quick overview of each tool:

TOOL 1: LAST WILL AND TESTAMENT

A will is a legal document that becomes effective as soon as you die. In your will, you can state who you want to receive your assets, have custody of your minor children, and be in charge of carrying out your instructions after you are gone. After you pass, your will is filed with the local court and enforced through a system called probate.

TOOL 2: ETHICAL WILL

An ethical will is a personal document or recording that communicate your beliefs, values, and legacy. It allows you to send public and personal messages upon your death, and it can include instructions about your burial and funeral. It is also a great way to remind others of shared memories. Although ethical wills aren't legally binding, they are an essential tool in your relational estate plan.

TOOL 3: ESTATE GUIDE AND INVENTORIE

An estate guide and inventory is a practical document that includes details that will make your personal representative's life easier and ease burdens for your loved ones when you are gone. At a minimum, it should include an inventory of your assets and contact information for the people who can help your personal representative carry out your relational estate plan.

TOOL 4: TRUST

Similar to a will, a trust is another option for transferring your asset after you die. However, a trust is much more flexible than a will. And unlike a will, you can establish a trust and transfer assets to it before you die, avoiding the probate process. The trust can continue long after you have passed, giving you the ability to control how your assets are used for years after you are gone. Also, unlike a will, a trust does not have to be filed with a court, which allows you to keep your estate plan private.

TOOL 5: BENEFICIARY DESIGNATION

Beneficiary designations are instructions you put on a bank account, investment account, retirement account, or insurance policy. When you die, the bank or insurance company will pay the money in that account or that policy to the person you have named. If you name a beneficiary on an account or policy, it will go to that beneficiary regardless of what your will or trust says and without going through the probate process.

TOOL 6: GIFTS AND MEMORIES LIST

A gifts and memories list is also sometimes referred to as a personal property memorandum. This document allows you to give specific personal items to certain people. Rather than including these gifts in your will or trust, which is very difficult to change, you can use the more accessible and adaptable gifts and memories list. Even better, it allows you to include background or stories about the gifts to help preserve special memories or impart your legacy.

TOOL 7: PLANNED GIVING

Planned giving is giving to charities at or after your death. It is a unique and powerful way to leave a legacy with the bonus of avoiding certain taxes.

TOOL 8: FUNERAL ARRANGEMENTS AND DIRECTIVE

Funeral directives are legal documents that give instructions about your funeral and burial. A funeral directive also allows you to pick someone who will be in charge of your funeral and burial. If there is a dispute, a funeral directive can be enforced by a court. By contrast, funeral arrangements are not legal documents and not enforceable. However, similar to funeral directives, they allow you to give instructions about your funeral and burial.

The chapters in this section will go into detail about what each of these tools are and how they funtion. Each chapter also contains several practical tips for using the tool as part of a relational estate plan. Let's start with the last will and testament.

CHAPTER 6:

LAST WILL AND TESTAMENT

"AT THE END OF THEIR LIVES, PEOPLE ASSESS HOW THEY'VE DONE NOT IN TERMS OF THEIR INCOME BUT IN TERMS OF THEIR SPIRIT, AND I BEG YOU TO DO THE SAME, EVEN IF THOSE WHO CAME BEFORE SOMETIMES FAILED TO DO SO."

–Anna Quindlen

No matter who you are, the presence or absence of a last will and testament is going to affect you either positively or negatively at some point. It is one of those things you can put off without any consequences until the day someone desperately needs it-and they'll either be thanking heaven you took the time to write a will, or they'll be wishing with all their heart you had. This is why a will is the first tool that is absolutely non-negotiable in a relational estate plan.

Some people create wills when they are young. Worried parents expecting their first baby come to our office to make a plan. With a new sense of responsibility about the future, these couples want to make a plan so they can sleep better at night knowing their child will be cared for should the worst happen.

Others create wills in their twilight years, knowing they have little time left. Elderly men and women come to our office, leaning on their children for support and carrying records of their assets in worn notebooks. They want the peace of knowing that everything they've worked so hard for will be passed into the right hands when they are gone.

Still others, of all ages, intend to write a will, but continue to put it off for one reason or another. Then, suddenly, it's too late. They die without a will, and their families pay the price of confusion, frustration, and conflict, on top of grief.

This last scenario happened to Bob. We never met him, but we met his daughter, Shelly. Bob had been Shelly's sole caretaker and provider because Shelly had severe physical disabilities that prevented her from working or even moving around some days. Because of her disabilities, she had qualified for and was receiving benefits from Medicaid and Social Security Disability. She told us that Bob had been working on a will but had never completed it. Unfortunately, without a will, Bob's assets were distributed according to the default rules in the state where he lived. These rules required that his assets be distributed equally between his two children, Shelly, and her estranged brother, John. John hadn't spoken to anyone in the family in 30 years. But after hearing that he would get some of Bob's money, he quickly showed up and began making unreasonable demands. This led to a year-long lawsuit between Shelly and Bob. To make matters even worse, the funds Shelly eventually received disqualified her from receiving additional Medicaid services. So at the end of the day, Bob's failure to create a will reduced the amount of funds Shelly received, gave money to a son who had abandoned the family, created a major conflict between Shelly and her brother, and disqualified Shelly from receiving Medicaid services she desperately needed. While we were able to mitigate some of these problems, it was still a catastrophe by anyone's definition. Bob and Shelly's situation illustrates why every relational estate plan should include a will. In this chapter, we will explore what a will is, how it can be used in a relational estate plan, and some practical tips when using wills.

Put simply, a will is a legal document that specifies where you want your assets to go when you die. After you pass, the instructions in the will are carried out by someone you appoint, called an executor or personal representative. A court reviews what your personal representative does to ensure that it complies with your instructions in the will. This whole process is called probate.

Wills vary widely from person to person and state to state, but most wills have four parts:

- instructions about paying expenses or debts
- instructions about what to do with assets
- appointment of personal representative
- signature and notary provisions.

None of these are as complicated as they may sound. Let's look at each part.

REQUIREMENT FOR PAYMENT OF EXPENSES

Almost every will begins with instructions about how to handle expenses, such as debts, taxes, funeral fees, and burial fees at your death. There are two reasons for this. First, it's the law. You must pay debts and expenses before you can leave assets to anyone else. Second, leaving these things unpaid will most likely mean that any creditors will try and collect the debts from your loved ones. While they may not succeed, it will be unpleasant for the people close to you.

INSTRUCTIONS ABOUT ASSETS

Next is instructions about what to do with the "residue," meaning what's left of your assets after the payment of your debts, expenses, and any specific gifts. This section explains the nitty-gritty of exactly who gets what. We call these people beneficiaries. They can be family members, friends, or organizations, such as a charity.

APPOINTMENT AND AUTHORITY OF PERSONAL REPRESENTATIVE

Third, wills normally have a section where a personal representative is appointed and given broad authority to carry out your wishes. This is also the section where a guardian can be appointed to care for minor children if both parents die. We recommend you choose multiple backups for both the personal representative and the guardian in case your first choice is unable to step into their role at the time of your death.

SIGNATURE AND NOTARY

The last section of a will is the signature and notary pages. Although the requirements vary from state to state, this section normally contains statements and signatures by you, witnesses, and a notary. If the will is written correctly, these statements and signatures will satisfy all the rules that your state requires for a will to be valid.

HOW A WILL CAN ACCOMPLISH THE GOALS OF RELATIONAL ESTATE PLANNING

In some estate plans, your will is the primary means of transferring your assets, while in others such as when you use a living trust, it serves as a backup. However you set things up, a will is crucial to your relational estate plan.

GOAL 1: A WILL PROTECTS AND PROVIDES FOR YOUR LOVED ONES

A will allows you to protect and provide for your loved ones by avoiding intestacy, using assets to meet needs, and appointing a guardian for minor children.

Intestacy is the legal term for the default rules that each state uses when someone dies without a will. Basically, the concept is this: if you don't put a plan in place for distributing your assets when you die, the state will use theirs-the intestacy rules. This is what happened to Bob and why Shelly had to split Bob's assets with her estranged brother.

Most people don't want the government's plan. The intestacy rules don't give you any control over your beneficiaries or personal representative. They almost always take longer to apply, cost more, and offer your loved ones less flexibility than a will. By creating a will, you remain in control of where your property goes when you die. And it probably goes without saying that you can't protect and provide for your loved ones if you don't control who gets what when you are gone.

A will also permits you to add conditions to gifts. For example, you may only want a beneficiary to receive something if all of your assets are more than a certain amount or if your beneficiary(s) has met some other condition, such as remaining in school or staying drug-free. A will allows you to impose conditions like these on what your beneficiaries receive. You can use these conditions as backup plans. For example, most people add a condition that a beneficiary must outlive them to receive a gift under a will. Otherwise, the gift goes to another beneficiary who is still alive. All this freedom and flexibility makes it easier to meet your loved ones' financial needs using a will.

Keep in mind, however, that the more specific and detailed your will is, the more complicated it will be to enforce, the greater of a burden it will be on your loved ones, and the greater the risk for conflict. Also, because the future is always unpredictable and things may happen that you don't anticipate, some of your conditions may become irrelevant or even harmful.

If you have children under eighteen, the most important thing your will can do is name a guardian. "Guardian" is a legal term that means a substitute parent. If both parents die before your child reaches age 18, a court will appoint a guardian or guardians to raise them. If a will specifies who you want to be the guardian for your children, then a judge must respect your decision and appoint the person you have named (at least in Virginia). However, if a will does not name a guardian, then a judge can pick whoever they want to raise your children. Obviously, your child's guardian is an important decision. You don't want to leave it up to a judge, and with a will you don't have to.

GOAL 2: A WILL AVOIDS CONFLICT

You can also use a will to avoid conflict by selecting the right person to be your personal representative. As we discussed in Chapter 2, one of the characteristics of a relational estate plan is that it uses a personal representative who is trusted and will promote peace among your family members. If you don't specify a personal representative in your will, then a judge gets to pick your personal representative, and they may very well pick the wrong person.

GOAL 5: A WILL EASES BURDENS

Finally, you can use a will in your relational estate plan to ease burdens and make your personal representative's job easier. Under the default rules of probate (in Virginia), the personal representative does not have much flexibility in how they handle your assets. If they want to do something differently because it saves money or is what your beneficiaries want, they must obtain permission from a judge. This can be time-consuming and expensive. So, experienced attorneys write wills to give the personal representative much broader authority than the default rules. This makes your personal representative's job easier, the process shorter, and the cost lower.

PRACTICAL TIPS FOR USING A WILL IN RELATIONAL ESTATE PLANNING

As you think about how a will can be used in your relational estate plan, here are three practical tips:

TIP 1: MAKE SURE THE WILL MEETS THE LEGAL REQUIREMENTS

Every will has to meet strict legal requirements to be valid. These vary from state to state, but most of the time they include:

- a meeting where you sign the will in the presence of two witnesses
- a notary to notarize your signature and the witness's signatures
- an oath made by you and your witnesses at the time of the signing

Be careful to follow all the necessary requirements in your state, and if you aren't sure what the requirements are, find a good estate planning attorney to help you. We frequently see wills that do not meet the legal requirements. At best, this means that we have to track down witnesses who saw the will being signed and subpoena them to appear at a hearing. At worst, it means the will is worthless and cannot be used.

TIP 2: HAVE A PLAN FOR PROBATE

A will is enforced through the probate process, as we discussed in Chapter 5. Probate takes longer, costs more, and offers much less privacy than other methods of distributing your assets. Because of this, some people prefer to use a different method to transfer their assets. If you choose to use another method, it doesn't mean you shouldn't have a will-it's just that your will becomes your backup plan to whatever your primary method is. Whatever you do, you should have a plan to make sure that your estate will pass through probate as efficiently as possible.

TIP 3: CONSIDER OTHER TOOLS IF FLEXIBILITY IS NEEDED

We believe everyone should have a will. But that doesn't mean it's the perfect tool for every situation. Wills have limitations that you need to keep in mind. We have already talked about the legal requirements to create a will and the fact that wills must go through probate. Another limitation is that wills can only do things at one point in time, when you die. Your will can direct assets wherever you want at that one point in time, but you cannot use it to control assets after you are gone. You will need another tool, a trust, if this is important to you.

Also, the probate process is public. After you are gone, anyone can look up what your will said, what you owned, and what you did with your assets. If this is a concern for you, then you will need to use other tools to transfer your assets.

Despite these limitations, a last will and testament is foundational for everyone's relational estate plan. It's the first essential tool.

CHAPTER 6 SUMMARY

A last will and testament is a legal document that specifies where you want your assets to go when you die. It generally has four sections: repayment of debts and expenses, distribution of assets, appointment and authority of personal representative, and signature and notary.

The last will and testament accomplishes Goals 1, 2, and 5 of relational estate planning.

- Goal 1: It protects and provides for your loved ones by allowing you to avoid intestacy, use assets to meet needs, and name a guardian to care for minor children.

- Goal 2: It avoids conflict by allowing you to select a trusted person to be your personal representative.

- Goal 5: It eases burdens by giving your personal representative authority to implement your estate plan.

Our three tips for using a last will and testament are:

- Tip 1: Make sure the will meets all the legal requirements.

- Tip 2: Have a plan for probate.

- Tip 3: Consider other tools besides a will if flexibility is needed.

CHAPTER 7:

ETHICAL WILL

"DEATH IS A CHALLENGE. IT TELLS US NOT TO WASTE TIME... IT TELLS
US TO TELL EACH OTHER RIGHT NOW THAT WE LOVE EACH OTHER."

-Leo Buscaglia

Although many people have never heard of them, ethical wills
are an ancient concept with a rich heritage. Ethical wills origi-
nated as a Jewish tradition. Our first record of the custom is at
the end of Genesis, right before Jacob, one of the fathers of mod-
ern-day Israel, dies. Jacob, also called Israel in the passage below,
begins his ethical will by blessing and encouraging his son, Joseph,
and his grandsons.

> After this, Joseph was told, 'Behold, your father is ill. So he
> took with him his two sons, Manasseh and Ephraim. And
> it was told to Jacob, 'Your son Joseph has come to you.'
> Then Israel summoned his strength and sat up in bed...
>
> And he blessed Joseph and said, 'The God before
> whom my fathers Abraham and Isaac walked, the God
> who has been my shepherd all my life long to this day,
> the angel who has redeemed me from all evil, bless
> the boys; and in them let my name be carried on, and
> the name of my fathers Abraham and Isaac; and let
> them grow into a multitude in the midst of the earth.'
>
> Then [Jacob] said to Joseph, 'Behold, I am
> about to die, but God will be with you and will
> bring you again to the land of your fathers.'
> Then Jacob called his [other] sons and said, 'Gather
> yourselves together, that I may tell you what shall
> happen to you in the days to come. Assemble and

listen, O sons of Jacob, listen to Israel your father.'

-Genesis 48 and 49, various verses.

Jacob goes on to discuss each of his sons' lives, his relationship with them, and what will happen to them in the future. Throughout his speech, Jacob reinforces his beliefs that good and evil will be repaid and that God is the deliverer and helper. Jacob also describes his sons as the future twelve tribes of the nation of Israel, creating a vision for them and their descendants for centuries to come. When you read it, you can almost picture Jacob turning from son to son as he addresses each of them.

After speaking his last words to them, Jacob gives practical instructions about how and where he wants to be buried. And then:

> When Jacob finished commanding his sons, he drew up his feet into the bed and breathed his last and was gathered to his people.
>
> -Genesis 49:33

Jacob's descendants continued to use ethical wills. The Old Testament contains many examples of them, including ones given by Moses, Joshua, David, and Solomon. In fact, the Biblical books of Proverbs and Ecclesiastes can be considered ethical wills.

Just as Jacob did, each of these Jewish leaders sought to pass on instructions, advice, wisdom, encouragement, and lessons learned. Their last words were the moral heritage they left for their children, descendants, and fellow Israelites. Hence, these speeches and records came to be known as ethical wills. The word ethical comes from the Greek word *ethos*, which means the set of values, moral beliefs, guiding principles, or habits that define a person. An ethical will is the passing on of the set values that have made you who you are.

Ethical wills have consistently been used in Jewish communities over the last three millennia, but recently they've spread beyond Jewish culture. Today, ethical wills are used by people of all different races and religions to communicate with loved ones and create legacies. We believe that ethical wills are the most important tool in a relational estate plan. Ethical wills have the unique ability to allow you to leave an inheritance of what is truly important in life: your values, your purpose, and the morals that guided you. This is more valuable than any physical inheritance and is the most relational thing you can do in estate planning.

ETHICAL WILLS AND THE GOALS OF RELATIONAL ESTATE PLANNING

Ethical wills help accomplish the first four relational estate planning goals.

GOAL 1: ETHICAL WILLS PROTECT AND PROVIDE FOR LOVED ONES

Ethical wills are a great way for you to meet your loved one's emotional and functional needs. At its simplest, an ethical will can tell your family and friends that you loved them. But it's an opportunity for much more. You can seek forgiveness from those you've wronged, offer reconciliation to those who have wronged you, motivate those who are weary, or strengthen those who are suffering.

An ethical will is also the perfect place for you to share life lessons that you have learned so that others can avoid your mistakes and learn from your example. Solomon left a tremendous ethical will of this type in the book of Ecclesiastes. He uses it to describe how he chased pleasures to find satisfaction and happiness, only to discover it was all worthless. "Vanity of vanities, all is vanity," he says. Solomon ends the book with these words to his son: "The end of the matter; all has been heard. Fear God and keep his commandments, for this is the whole duty of man." (Ecclesiastes

12:13). Millennia later, we still sense the conviction and regret in Solomon's tone and hear his desire for his sons not to repeat his mistakes. This is one of an ethical will's great uses. It can protect those we love by helping them avoid the consequences we ourselves have faced.

GOAL 2: AN ETHICAL WILL CAN AVOID CONFLICT

An ethical will can also be used to avoid conflict. It gives you a chance to explain why you made certain decisions about your assets or appointed one person instead of another as your personal representative. We often see people get upset if they aren't named as the personal representative in a will. In truth, it's a hard job and requires a lot of work. In our experience, those who get angry or hurt over this issue aren't crazy. But they think that the person who died named people they loved or trusted the most. An ethical will can stop this kind of thinking by allowing you to explain why you made the choices you did. If you don't explain your choices, your family and friends will most likely jump to conclusions and may assume the worst.

GOAL 3: AN ETHICAL WILL LEAVES A LEGACY

An ethical will is a huge part of leaving a legacy. You can explain why you had certain interests and why you pursued certain goals. You can talk about your hobbies and why they were important to you. You can recount the charities that you supported and why you believed in them. But most importantly, you can leave your values, moral beliefs, and guiding principles. What did you believe in so strongly that you based the major decisions in your life on it? What did you dedicate your life to? What guided you through dark times?

If you are a person of faith, your legacy will almost certainly include your religious beliefs. An ethical will can be a great place to include a statement of faith. Statements of faith are sometimes included in a last will and testament. But we prefer to place them in ethical wills, since last wills and testaments are rarely read more than once, and even then, they are mainly used to determine who gets what. Ethical wills, on the other hand, are often read and reread many times as family heirlooms. If your faith is important to you, you want to make sure what you believed isn't tucked away into a corner and forgotten Here's an example of a Christian statement of faith:

> Looking forward to the time when my earthly life shall end, I wish to bear witness to Christ's completed work on the cross on my behalf (Hebrews 9:11-12). I have placed my faith and confidence in Jesus Christ and received his abundant grace (Ephesians 2:8-9, John 1:16). My old life has passed away and He has made me new (2 Corinthian 5:17). I will confidently (Hebrews 6:19-20, Hebrews 10:23) pass from this life into an eternity in the presence of my Lord, having my faith turned to sight. My deepest desire is for my family to know the Lord and to find Him sufficient for all their needs (2 Corinthians 12:9). It is my wish that my family would celebrate the life that the Lord gave me on this earth while having their eyes fixed, with expectant hope, on Christ and His promises. All of my earthly possessions belong to the Lord. For a season, I have managed and enjoyed what He has entrusted to me. My desire is that my loved ones will view all things as gifts from the Lord, including this earthly inheritance, and that they will trust Him in managing it.

Regardless of your faith, we hope you grasp the power that a statement like this can have. It not only explains your beliefs, but it encourages others to follow you. Passing on your belief system is a monumental part of leaving your legacy, and an ethical will is a great place to do it.

GOAL 4: AN ETHICAL WILL CAN PRESERVE MEMORIES

Reminding people of fond memories is another hallmark

of ethical wills. We have a dear friend whose family has taken vacations to a beach in South Carolina for the last twenty years. In her ethical will, she recounted some of her favorite stories and meaningful family moments of those vacations. What stories do you want others to remember when they think of you? What memories should not be forgotten? An ethical will can remind your loved ones of times you treasured together.

PRACTICAL TIPS FOR USING AN ETHICAL WILL IN RELATIONAL ESTATE PLANNING

There are no hard and fast rules for what you should include in an ethical will. But here are five practical tips to get you started.

TIP 1: JUST DO IT (THE ETHICAL WILL)

The first tip is the simplest, but also the most important. Force yourself to get started, and soon. In our experience, the ethical will is one thing that people put off, thinking they have plenty of time to do it. In the passage above, it seems Jacob had a sense of 'I can't die until I speak these last words to my sons.' It would be nice if we were all guaranteed to be able to speak noble words to our loved ones before we passed. But we don't all get that chance, which is why it's important that you write your ethical will sooner rather than later.

TIP 2: START THE ETHICAL WILL WITH WHO AND WHAT

It is very rare that an ethical will is written to everyone. Most of the time, it's directed to a specific loved one or group of loved ones. Think about who you want to make sure reads or hears your ethical will.

Once you have your list, think about each of them and what you want to tell them. Decide what you want each person to know. In

Section Three, we include a link to a guide to help you articulate important events, lessons, and discoveries of your life. We've included questions like: What life accomplishments are you most proud of? What was the most difficult thing you had to face in life, and what did you learn from it? What are you grateful for? Who significantly invested in you? Think along these lines to get your creative juices flowing.

TIP 3: AVOID BEING NEGATIVE IN YOUR ETHICAL WILL

Be careful with your words and tone in an ethical will; this is not a place to manipulate, criticize, or judge others. Seek to communicate what is important without being negative, regardless of tension you may have had in certain relationships. Your ethical will may exist long after your death, so use discernment. Only leave words your are sure you won't regret.

TIP 4: SEASON YOUR ADVICE IN THE ETHICAL WILL WITH EXPERIENCES

If you are like most of our clients, you have advice or thoughts for your family, friends, and community that you may want to include in your ethical will. That's great, but we suggest you also use your experiences to explain how you came to those beliefs or why you are making requests. The more you communicate your experiences, the less likely someone will be to assume what you are saying is controlling or paternal.

One of our clients, Sandra, was very concerned about her daughter, Emily, whose marriage was ending. Sandra had tried on multiple occasions to tell Emily that she needed to learn how to manage her own finances, rather than relying on her husband to do so. But Emily never took her mother's advice. When we first met Sandra, she had given up on the idea of ever getting through to Emily. However, we encouraged her to use an ethical will to explain why financial independence was so important to her. So,

Sandra wrote an ethical will that explaining where her high value on women understanding money came from. She reminded her daughter that she had been a single mother, and her mother had been a single mother. She explained to Emily how difficult it had been for both of them to raise their families. She recalled some painful and personal memories to illustrate that she knew firsthand the impact of both wise and unwise financial decisions. After sharing her heart, Sandra again requested that Emily take the time to educate herself financially.

Sandra didn't wait until she died for Emily to read the ethical will. She gave it to her as soon as she finished it. As she read it, Emily broke down in tears. She finally understood why this principle was so important to her mother after all that Sandra had lived through, and she promised to do as she asked. By including her own story as an explanation, Sandra's request became much more powerful.

TIP 5: BE CREATIVE ABOUT HOW YOU COMMUNICATE YOUR ETHICAL WILL

Lastly, don't forget to leave instructions for how your ethical will should be communicated. You can have it sent as a letter, read at your funeral, played as a video, or posted on social media. We read about one Jewish doctor from the 12th century who demanded that his son read his ethical will every day for the rest of the son's life. This is going too far, but most people today have the opposite problem-they don't provide any instructions. Make sure you take the time to think through the best way for your ethical will to be communicated and then include those suggestions in your estate plan.

At the end of the day, you know best what your family, friends, and community need to hear from you. Whatever the dynamics of your relationships, your goal with an ethical will should be to bring closure between you and others and to help them move forward into their future. Maybe you need to address and mend conflict. Maybe this is your chance to preserve those special, important memories. Maybe you need to give someone advice tailored specifically to where you see them headed in life. Maybe they just need to hear you're proud of them, that you love them. Whatever you say, we've found that the best ethical wills seem to have an unspoken message woven between their lines: 'This is who I was, this is who you were to me. This is who we were together. This is what I must say before I leave you.'

We are confident you won't regret creating an ethical will as part of your relational estate plan. And the joy, comfort, guidance, and love you'll bring to your relationships is a priceless gift that no physical inheritance could ever match.

CHAPTER 7 SUMMARY

An ethical will is a non-legal document that allows you to communicate your beliefs, values, experiences, and advice to your family, friends, and community. It is the most important tool of relational estate planning.

An ethical will accomplishes Goals 1, 2, 3, and 4 of relational estate planning.

- Goal 1: It protects and provides for your loved ones by meeting their functional and emotional needs.

- Goal 2: It avoids conflict by explaining your choices and decisions.

- Goal 3: It leaves a legacy by stating your values and beliefs.

- Goal 4: It preserves memories by reminding others of them.

Our five tips for creating an ethical will:

- Tip 1: Just do it. (The ethical will).

- Tip 2: Start the ethical will with who and what.

- Tip 3: Avoid being negative in your ethical will.

- Tip 4: Season your advice in the ethical will with experiences.

- Tip 5: Be creative about how you communicate your ethical will.

CHAPTER 8:

ESTATE GUIDE AND INVENTORY

"AN IDEA CAN ONLY BECOME A REALITY ONCE IT IS BROKEN DOWN
INTO ORGANIZED, ACTIONABLE ELEMENTS."

*-Scott Belsky, "Making Ideas Happen: Overcoming the Obstacles Between
Vision and Reality"*

The third and final essential tool in any relational estate plan is the estate guide and inventory. In this chapter, we will go over what the estate guide and inventory should include, how it can be used in a relational estate plan, and some practical tips for using it well.

Mary recently contacted us with a familiar story. Her uncle had died. He was a bit of a recluse, and no one in the family knew where he had his bank accounts, let alone what other assets he owned. He was also a hoarder. Mary and her siblings were completely overwhelmed, and the fact that they couldn't find his bank accounts just made a bad situation that much worse. She asked the question we've heard a hundred times, "How do we find his assets?"

Unfortunately for her and many people in her situation, there isn't a database that keeps a record of everything a person owns. The only thing we could tell her was to play the "mailbox game." The mailbox game is not fun, and it's not a game. It's an annoying exercise we've seen too many families go through. They wait for the deceased person's mail to come and look for bank and investment statements, hoping to piece together what their family member owned. It takes a long time, especially for accounts that only send out annual statements, and it doesn't work for everything. More and more accounts send out electronic rather than paper statements, and unless you happen to have someone's email username and password, it's difficult, if not impossible, to access their email and get these statements. It is this nightmare that the estate guide and inventory is meant to avoid. It normally includes three parts: an inventory of your assets, initial instructions, and a list of key contacts.

INVENTORY OF YOUR ASSETS

The first part of an estate guide and inventory is a list of your assets, where they are located, and how to access them. Here are a few common things that are normally included in this section: bank and investment accounts, insurance policies, location of tangible assets, such as valuable collectibles or jewelry, location of titles and deeds, locations and contents of safety deposit boxes, online account logins and passwords, passwords for electronic devices, and contact information for creditors, such as mortgages, credit cards, and car loans.

Keep in mind that state and federal laws govern who can access your accounts after you have passed, and it can be illegal in some instances for your loved ones to access your online information after you are gone, even if they have your login and password. If you have questions about these laws, we recommend you speak with an estate planning attorney in your state.

INSTRUCTIONS

Next, your estate guide and inventory should include instructions about two things. The first is the ongoing maintenance of your assets. Are there things you own that need ongoing maintenance or care? The second section explains how to implement your relational estate plan. What will your personal representative need to know to implement your plan?

LIST OF KEY ADVISORS

The last component of an estate guide and inventory is a list of key contacts. Attorneys, financial advisors, accountants, bankers, insurance agents, and funeral homes should all be on the list along with anyone else that your loved ones might need to contact.

HOW THE ESTATE GUIDE AND INVENTORY CAN ACCOMPLISH THE GOALS OF RELATIONAL ESTATE PLANNING

While the estate guide and inventory is designed primarily to ease burdens, it also protects and provides for loved ones and preserves memories.

GOAL 1: AN ESTATE GUIDE AND INVENTORY PROTECTS AND PROVIDES FOR YOUR LOVED ONES.

As we discussed in Chapter 1, meeting functional needs is a key part of protecting and providing for your loved ones. The estate guide and inventory allows you to meet these functional needs with detailed instructions about what practical details or things your family or friends will need to know.

This is particularly true if you are the caregiver for someone who cannot communicate. We heard the story of one young man who lived with and cared for his grandfather, who was deaf and dumb. Tragically, the young man found out he had cancer and did not have long to live. He found a nursing home that would take his grandfather and made all the financial arrangements. But, in addition to those, he also left the nursing home a letter telling them about his grandfather's likes and dislikes. He wrote down small details he knew would bring his gradnfather joy. He told them that his grandfather's favorite dessert was raisin pie with vanilla ice cream, that he loved bird-watching and would be thrilled to have a birdfeeder near his window, and that his knees often bothered him. This is a great example of how you can meet a functional need with an estate guide and inventory.

GOAL 4: AN ESTATE GUIDE AND INVENTORY PRESERVES MEMORIES

A few years ago, we knew a young man (we'll call him Nate) whose wife died very suddenly, leaving him a single father of three little girls, each of whom struggled deeply with losing their mother. Of all her possessions, the most meaningful thing to Nate and his daughters were her photos of them as a family. Unfortunately, all of the photos she had taken were locked in her Amazon account. Nate knew the username, but didn't have the password, so Amazon wouldn't give him the photos. He fought with them for over a year and filed two different lawsuits to try and force Amazon to give him access to those photos. While he was finally successful, it was a problem and a cost he should never have had to deal with while mourning the loss of his wife. An estate guide and inventory allows you to avoid the problems that Nate faced and preserve memories for your loved ones by providing them with all the information they need.

GOAL 5: AN ESTATE GUIDE AND INVENTORY EASES BURDENS

Finally and most importantly, a well-written estate guide and inventory eases burdens for your loved ones. It provides them with key information they will need instead of forcing them to find it on their own, as happened to Mary at the beginning of this chapter. We can't tell you how many problems, difficulties, tears, frustrations, and even fights would have been avoided had the deceased simply provided a list of assets or a few practical instructions.

Now that we have gone through how an estate guide and inventory fits into a relational estate plan, here are a few practical tips on using them.

PRACTICAL TIPS FOR USING AN ESTATE GUIDE AND INVENTORY

TIP 1: CONSIDER USING A PASSWORD MANAGER AS PART OF THE ESTATE GUIDE AND INVENTORY

With all the online accounts most of us have, most of the information your loved ones will need to access will be in electronic form. While you can keep all the passwords written down in a physical notebook or electronic document, you should at least consider a password manager. A password manager is a program that stores your passwords electronically. You have one universal password that allows access to all your other usernames and passwords. By using this as part of your estate guide and inventory, you can reduce the list of usernames and passwords you need to include in the estate guide and inventory. Even better, the password manager can automatically keep the list of usernames and passwords updated for you, which leads us to the next tip.

TIP 2: UPDATE THE ESTATE GUIDE AND INVENTORY REGULARLY

Since it is practical day-to-day living document, the estate guide and inventory is the most likely document to become outdated as your life changes. To maintain your relational estate plan, you will need to review and update the estate guide and inventory regularly. We recommend you plan to do this every year, and when special occasions call for it, such as when you move or change jobs or financial institutions.

TIP 3: INCLUDE DETAILED INSTRUCTIONS IN THE ESTATE GUIDE AND INVENTORY

Do not skip the instructions section of your estate guide and inventory! Your loved ones will need a lot of direction. For example, do you have regular commitments? Caring for pets, paying a mortgage, serving at a local charity? Which vet do you use? When is the mortgage due? What does the charity depend on you to do? Your loved ones will also need instructions about how to deal with your estate. Where will you be buried? Where are your funeral arrangements? What is your plan for dealing with probate? How do you want your ethical will distributed? All these things and more should be spelled out in the instructions section of your estate guide and inventory. By including detailed instructions, you can both avoid unnecessary anxiety and stress for your family and friends and make sure they know how to implement your relational estate plan.

TIP 4: THINK BROADLY ABOUT IMPORTANT CONTACTS FOR THE ESTATE GUIDE AND INVENTORY

Our final tip is to think broadly about the people who can help your loved ones deal with your estate. In the list above, we included some of the obvious ones, such as attorneys, accountants, and financial advisors. But we encourage you to think of others who could help. For example, if your personal representative will most likely have to sell your house, do you know a good realtor? If they will need to sell a business, is there a broker who might be able to find a buyer quickly? These professionals can help your loved ones navigate the legal, financial, and practical steps after your death and keep them from making mistakes.

We meet so many people who didn't have this information, made a simple mistake, and became stuck heading down the wrong path in dealing with a loved one's estate. We've seen personal representatives become liable for the deceased's debts and houses foreclosed unnecessarily. We have even seen people go through probate when they didn't have to. Each of these could have been prevented by a quick conversation with the right professional. So, make sure you include contact information for anyone who might be helpful to your loved ones in the estate guide and inventory.

It might take some time, but creating your estate guide and inventory is worth the heavy lifting now to protect your loved ones from unnecessary pain later. It will make the administration of your estate quicker, easier, and simpler for whoever gets the job.

CHAPTER 8 SUMMARY

An estate guide and inventory is the third and final tool that should be used in every relational estate plan. It is a practical, non-legal document that is designed to aid your loved ones after your death. It normally includes an inventory of your assets, initial instructions, and key contacts.

An estate guide and inventory helps you accomplish Goals 1, 4, and 5 in your relational estate plan.

- Goal 1: It protects and provides for your loved ones by helping you meet their functional needs after you are gone.

- Goal 4: It preserves memories by making sure loved ones have access to important pictures and other digital files.

- Goal 5: It eases burdens by providing your loved ones with important information and key contact.

Our four tips for using an estate guide and inventory are:

- Tip 1: Consider using a password manager as part of the estate guide and inventory.

- Tip 2: Update the estate guide and inventory regularly.

- Tip 3: Include detailed instructions in the estate guide and inventory.

- Tip 4: Think broadly about important contacts for the estate guide and inventory.

CHAPTER 9:

TRUST

"DEATH ENDS A LIFE, NOT A RELATIONSHIP."
-Mitch Albom, "Tuesdays with Morrie"

When you research estate planning, the legal terms can start to get confusing. People often confuse trusts and wills, as it can be hard to know the difference between them and what each one does. In this chapter, we're going to define what trusts are and then consider how you can use them as part of a relational estate plan. We will end with several practical tips for using trusts well.

Think of a trust as a fake person that you create. A trust can own property, buy and sell things, and even own and run a business. A trust operates according to rules that you set up and is overseen by someone you pick, called a trustee. All these rules must be in the written form of a trust agreement.

You may have heard the terms living, *inter-vivos*, testamentary, revocable, or irrevocable used in connection with trusts. Living trusts are also called *inter-vivos* trusts. *Inter-vivos* is Latin for "between the living." This kind of trust begins operating while you are still living. Testamentary trusts, on the other hand, don't take effect until your death. In a revocable trust, you reserve the right to change the trust if you need or want to. An irrevocable trust, however, cannot be changed once you make it.

Trusts are very flexible tools. Depending on your goals, the trust you use may have a completely different purpose and a different set of rules for how it operates than someone else's trust. But the basic idea for all trusts is the same: the person who benefits from the money in the trust (the beneficiary) is different from the person who makes decisions about the money in the trust (the trustee). You are giving the trustee, not the beneficiary, the right to decide how the money in the trust should be used for the beneficiary.

TRUSTS VS. WILLS

Should you have a trust or a will? As with many aspects of estate planning, the answer to this question depends on you, your loved ones, and your goals. Generally, trusts are more complicated, more expensive, and more difficult to maintain than wills. But trusts are also more flexible than wills, and they're private, whereas a will becomes part of the public record after you die. The question is also a bit misleading, since when you use a trust, you should still have a will as part of your plan.

With all this being said, the short answer to this question is that you should use a trust when a will by itself cannot accomplish all of the goals for your relational estate plan.

HOW A TRUST CAN ACCOMPLISH THE GOALS OF RELATIONAL ESTATE PLANNING

You can use a trust in a relational estate plan to:

- Protect and provide for loved ones by meeting financial needs.
- Leave a legacy or preserve memories by paying for activities or other things after death.
- Ease burdens by avoiding the probate process.

GOAL 1: A TRUST PROTECTS AND PROVIDES FOR LOVED ONES BY MEETING FINANCIAL NEEDS

While you can use a last will and testament to specify who will get your assets after your death, a will doesn't allow you to control what they do with those assets. A trust, on the other hand, allows you to control how someone uses your assets after you are gone. Here are several specific situations in which it may make sense to use a trust to control your assets after you are gone.

PROTECTING MINOR CHILDREN

The most common reason people use a trust to control assets is to prevent children from wasting their inheritance. If you leave money to a minor child in a will, they will receive it as soon as they turn 18. But most 18-year-olds are not ready to handle large amounts of money. Several studies have confirmed that young adults who receive an early inheritance are much more likely to struggle with depression, anxiety, substance abuse, and even suicide.

By using a trust, you can place restrictions on a child's use of their funds. Until they are older, the trustee oversees the money and uses it to meet your child's financial needs, including living expenses, healthcare, education, and travel.

DEALING WITH BLENDED FAMILIES

A trust can also be used to control assets for non-traditional or blended families. For example, if your current spouse is not the parent of your children, you may want to make sure your current spouse is cared for while they are alive but not give them complete control over your funds. Even if you are confident your spouse will use your funds well, you still may want to put restrictions on how they use your money, in case, as they get older, someone else takes control of their finances.

PROVIDING FOR LOVED ONES WHO MAKE POOR DECISIONS

Sadly, many clients need to provide for a loved one who does not make wise financial decisions. You can use a trust in this situation so that your resources can't be used for substance abuse, wasteful spending, or other destructive patterns. Instead, you can require that your money only be spent on certain things that are approved by the trustee. You can also limit the amount of funds that a loved one receives each month or each year to prevent them from spending everything at once.

CARING FOR DISABLED LOVED ONES

Finally, trusts can be used to control assets when caring for disabled family members. This type of trust is called a special needs trust, and it is critical when dealing with someone who is receiving government entitlements. Government entitlements, such as Social Security Disability Insurance and Medicaid, have financial qualifications. In other words, you need to earn less and own less than a certain amount to qualify. If you give someone who is receiving these entitlements even a modest sum of money, you could disqualify them from future benefits. A special needs trust allows you to set money aside to be used for a loved one, but it does not give them ownership or control over that money. If it is set up correctly, the loved one gets the benefit of the funds and continues to receive their government benefits.

GOALS 3 AND 4: A TRUST CAN LEAVE A LEGACY AND PRESERVE MEMORIES

There are many ways you can use a trust creatively to remind others of your legacy or preserve special memories. Remember our friends who valued family relationships and set aside money to pay for family vacations after they were gone? They used a trust to manage the money and pay for vacations.

A trust can be used to encourage your family or friends to revisit places you went together or to set aside funds to allow them to pursue a hobby you enjoyed together. We know of several families that also used trusts to encourage education and giving. In one instance, a high school math teacher who had no children set up a trust to encourage students from her school to go to college. Each year, the faculty at the school select the best math student to receive a college scholarship. That teacher's legacy of education is supported by the trust she left behind.

GOAL 5: A TRUST EASES BURDENS BY AVOIDING PROBATE

As we discussed earlier, probate is the process courts use to enforce a person's will once they die. Probate can be expensive, time-consuming, and difficult. One way you can ease burdens for your loved ones is to set up an estate plan that avoids this process. A revocable, living trust is the most common way to avoid probate, and it works like this. When you die, most of the things you own must go through probate before they can be distributed to your loved ones. However, a trust is a separate legal person. When you transfer your assets to a trust, you no longer technically own them. The trust does. If you do this with all your assets, then there is nothing to go through probate when you die. Instead, those assets can be distributed quickly and easily through the trust, without the burden or oversight of the probate process. When we set up this type of trust, we normally provide that the person who created the trust remains in control of the trust until they die. After they die, a new trustee steps in to carry out the instructions for distributing the trust assets to their loved ones.

PRACTICAL TIPS FOR USING A TRUST IN RELATIONAL ESTATE PLANNING

TIP 1: ONLY USE A TRUST IF IT FITS IN YOUR RELATIONAL ESTATE PLAN

We frequently see many people who view a trust as some sort of status symbol or indication of wealth or sophistication. But, as with every tool of relational estate planning, you should only use a trust if you need it to accomplish your relational estate planning goals. If you can accomplish those goals without a trust, skip it.

TIP 2: AVOID UNNECESSARY DETAIL IN TRUSTS

Almost every month, we meet a new client who brings in their old estate documents in a huge binder. In almost all of these cases, they have an old trust agreement that is more than 50 pages long. Few people need a trust this complicated. While it may seem harmless to include dozens of pages of legal boilerplate in your trust agreement, it isn't. Your loved ones are much more likely to have conflict with each other if your trust is hard to understand. And, your trustee will have to spend much more time dealing with a large, convoluted trust agreement than one that is smaller and tailored to your specific needs. Even worse, if you and your advisors aren't careful, the boilerplate could interfere with the rest of your estate plan. So, make sure your trust only contains instructions your trustee will use.

TIP 3: FOR TRUSTS TO AVOID PROBATE, MAKE SURE YOUR ASSETS ARE CORRECTLY TITLED AND REVIEWED REGULARLY

If you are using a trust to avoid probate, you need to make sure that your assets are correctly titled in the name of the trust or you have some other method to avoid probate. This is because you can only avoid probate if you don't technically own any assets when you die. If you forget even one asset, your loved ones could be forced to go through the whole probate process. This happened to my (Josh's) grandmother. She created an estate plan which was designed to avoid probate. It included a revocable trust, and for years, she kept all her assets correctly titled in the name of the trust. However, when she was 97 years old, she accidentally retitled one certificate of deposit, or CD, into her own name. When she died, her executor had to spend over a year going through the probate process for that one CD. If your plan includes using a revocable trust to avoid probate, you need to make that your assets stay correctly titled, and this means reviewing everything regularly.

CHAPTER 9 SUMMARY

A trust is a helpful tool in several different scenarios. It can protect and provide for a loved one without giving that loved one control over their money. It can also be used to keep an estate plan private and avoid probate.

A trust can be used to accomplish Goals 1, 3, 4, and 5 of relational estate planning.

- Goal 1: A trust can protect and provide for loved ones by meeting financial needs in a controlled fashion.

- Goals 3 and 4: A trust can encourage others to remember your legacy or relive special memories.

- Goal 5: A trust can ease burdens by avoiding the probate process.

Our tips for trusts are:

- Tip 1: Only use a trust if it fits in your relational estate plan.

- Tip 2: Avoid unnecessary detail in trusts.

- Tip 3: For trusts to avoid probate, make sure your assets are correctly titled and reviewed regularly.

CHAPTER 10:

BENEFICIARY DESIGNATION

"SOMETIMES THE POOREST MAN LEAVES HIS CHILDREN THE RICHEST
INHERITANCE."

-Ruth E. Renkel

Beneficiary designations are a unique option among the eight estate planning tools. They aren't documents you create for yourself. Rather, they are instructions you give to your bank or financial institution to transfer your accounts to a certain person or persons when you pass. Beneficiary designations work independently of your will or trust, and the bank will follow the beneficiary designations regardless of what your will or your trust says.

DIFFERENT TYPES OF BENEFICIARY DESIGNATIONS

There are two types of beneficiary designations, and the one you use will depend on the type of account you have. A payable on death, or POD, designation is self-explanatory. When you die, the bank or financial institution pays your beneficiary the value of the funds (or other assets) in the account. These designations are used on most checking, savings, and other cash accounts. However, they normally are not used on accounts that contain assets other than cash, such as stocks, bonds, and other financial investments.

A transfer on death, or TOD, designation means that your assets in a particular account will be transferred to your beneficiary when you die. They will not be sold, but retitled. This designation is used for retirement or investment accounts that own stocks, bonds, and investments. Normally, the owners don't want these assets sold. So, they use a TOD designation to transfer them directly to their heirs when they die.

HOW BENEFICIARY DESIGNATIONS CAN ACCOMPLISH THE GOALS OF RELATIONAL ESTATE PLANNING

You can use beneficiary designations as part of your relational estate plan in three different ways:

- Goal 1: Protect and provide for loved ones by avoiding taxes on tax-deferred funds.
- Goal 2: Avoid conflict by transferring assets privately.
- Goal 5: Ease burdens by avoiding probate.

GOAL 1: A BENEFICIARY DESIGNATION PROTECTS AND PROVIDES FOR YOUR LOVED ONES BY AVOIDING TAXES ON TAX DEFERRED FUNDS

Even though relational estate planning isn't primarily about the amount of money you leave behind, no one wants to pay the government more than necessary. The more money you keep, the more you'll have to protect and provide for your loved ones. You can refer to Chapter 17 for more details on how taxes will impact your estate, but for now, understand that tax-deferred funds such as 401ks and individual retirment accounts or traditional IRAs are normally taxed less if they are transferred directly to someone with a beneficiary designation instead of going through a will and the probate process.

GOAL 2: BENEFICIARY DESIGNATIONS AVOID CONFLICTS BY TRANSFERRING ASSETS PRIVATELY

Beneficiary designations are also popular because they are private, even more so than trusts. You might remember that wills, once they are recorded, become public and that probate is also a public process. This means that after you die and your estate goes through probate, anyone can find out exactly what you owned and who you left it to. Trusts are much more private; but still, in many states, anyone who is a beneficiary under a trust has the right to read the trust agreement. Beneficiary designations are more private than wills or trusts. In our experience, banks and other financial institutions will only disclose information about the account with the beneficiary designation to the beneficiary themselves. This means you can use a beneficiary designation to leave a loved one certain money or assets without anyone else knowing about it. Only the beneficiary will be able to learn what you left them. Because of this, you need to make sure your beneficiaries know about the accounts ahead of time.

GOAL 3: BENEFICIARY DESIGNATIONS EASE BURDENS BY AVOIDING PROBATE

We've already talked about trusts as one option for avoiding probate and easing the burdens on your loved ones. Beneficiary designations are another way to avoid probate. They transfer the funds directly to your beneficiaries, which means the funds don't go through probate. This needs to be done carefully for reasons we'll get into below, but beneficiary designations are frequently used as part of a plan to avoid probate.

PRACTICAL TIPS FOR USING BENEFICIARY DESIGNATIONS IN RELATIONAL ESTATE PLANNING

As you think about how you can use beneficiary designations, keep these tips in mind:

TIP 1: COMPLY WITH THE FINANCIAL INSTITUTIONS REQUIREMENTS FOR BENEFICIARY DESIGNATIONS

Each financial institution has different requirements for using beneficiary designations on their accounts. You want to make sure that you understand and comply with these requirements. If you don't, your assets may not be transferred where you want or could even go through probate.

TIP 2: UNDERSTAND THE LIMITATIONS OF BENEFICIARY DESIGNATIONS BEFORE YOU USE THEM.

Beneficiary designations can be wonderful if used in the right situation, but before you decide if they are right for your estate plan, understand that they come with several drawbacks.

First, beneficiary designations only have one level of backups. Let's say you have an account where the beneficiary is your spouse and the contingent or backup beneficiary is your son. What if you want to name your cousin as a backup to your son? You can't. If tragedy were to occur and both your spouse and child died before you, the beneficiary designation would not apply, and the money would pass through probate. Wills and trusts, by contrast, allow more than one level of backup beneficiaries.

Second, you can't put conditions on beneficiary designations. For example, if you only want money paid to a child when they have reached a certain age, a beneficiary designation won't let you do it. You will have to use a will or a trust to set up any type of condition.

Third, beneficiary designations are not subject to court oversight. This means that the bank or financial institution makes the final decision about who gets your money. If there is a mistake, there is nothing your loved ones can do. But if someone makes a mistake with a will or a trust, your heirs or personal representative can take the matter to court to review the error and hopefully get it sorted out.

And fourth, you can't use beneficiary designations for real property or physical possessions, only financial assets. This is why beneficiary designations have to be used in tandem with a will or trust.

Make sure you keep these drawbacks in mind as you think about beneficiary designations.

TIP 3: MAKE SURE BENEFICIARIES KNOW THE ACCOUNTS THEY WILL RECEIVE

After you have died, banks will normally refuse to tell anyone about an account with a beneficiary designation, except the beneficiary. Sometimes, they won't even admit that the account exists. So, if you don't tell the beneficiary about the account before your death, it can be difficult for them to locate and gain access to the funds you left for them.

We once knew an elderly man who decided to plan his estate using only payable on death designations on savings accounts. He wanted to leave his assets to his four sisters and had listed them each as beneficiaries on a different account. The problem was, each account was at a different bank, and he didn't tell anyone about his plan. It created a nightmare when he died. No one knew what was where. His sisters had to go to all the local banks, individually step up to the counter, and ask, "Am I the beneficiary on this account?" until the right sister hit the right account at the right bank. On top of all that, his sisters lived in three different states and were forced to travel several times to sort it out. It's a little comical to picture, but it wasn't funny at the time.

TIP 4: KEEP GOOD RECORDS SO YOU DON'T FORGET ABOUT YOUR BENEFICIARY DESIGNATIONS

Since you need a separate beneficiary designation for each account, it can be easy to lose track of one or forget to change it. There are many stories of former spouses receiving funds that were clearly not intended for them because someone forgot to change a beneficiary designation. If you intend to use beneficiary designations, make sure you keep good records so you can remember to change them when you update your plan.

CHAPTER 10 SUMMARY

A beneficiary designation is an instruction to financial institution about who they should give your financial accounts or assets to when you die. There are two types of beneficiary designations: payable on death, which pays the money in the account to someone, and transfer on death, which transfers the financial assets in the account (such as stocks and bonds) to someone.

Beneficiary designations can be used to accomplish Goals 1, 2, and 5 of Relational Estate Planning:

- Goal 1: They protect and provide for your loved ones by allowing you to avoid taxes on tax-deferred funds.

- Goal 2: They avoid conflict by allowing you to transfer assets privately.

- Goal 5: They ease burdens by avoiding probate for certain assets.

Our four tips for using beneficiary designations are:

- Tip 1: Comply with the financial institution's requirements for naming a beneficiary designation on an account.

- Tip 2: Understand the limitations of beneficiary designations before you use them.

- Tip 3: Make sure your beneficiaries know which accounts they are designees on.

- Tip 4: Keep good records so you don't forget to update your accounts.

TOOL 6: GIFTS AND MEMORIES LIST

"I'VE LEARNED THAT PEOPLE WILL FORGET WHAT YOU SAID, PEOPLE WILL FORGET WHAT YOU DID, BUT PEOPLE WILL NEVER FORGET HOW YOU MADE THEM FEEL."

-Maya Angelou

We've covered several tools for leaving your financial assets to certain people, but for specific personal items, you will want to use a different method. Although you can list physical assets in a will or a trust, we don't recommend it. A will is not easy to change once it has been signed and notarized. You cannot handwrite changes into it, so even small amendments are a hassle. They must be carried out in the same way as the original document: with a notary, witnesses, oaths, and so on. Trusts are a little easier to change, but even they require a written amendment, which should be drafted by your attorney, meaning more money and time on your part. More than that, these items are much more likely to have an emotional meaning or story attached to them, and you need to ensure it gets passed on. This is where a gifts and memories list comes in.

HOW THE GIFTS AND MEMORIES LIST WORKS

A gifts and memories list is a written list of personal property gifts separate from your will or trust. Your will or trust should mention, but not include, the gifts and memories list. In many states, this makes the gifts and memories list enforceable as part of your will or trust, but also makes it much easier to be changed. For example, in Virginia, the only requirements are that the list be referred to by your will, signed by you (witnesses and notaries are not required), and limited to personal property. The gifts and memories list cannot be used with land or financial accounts.

Your gifts and memories list should name specific items, along with the person you want to receive each item, and the story or history behind each item. While the story or history of an item is not required, we encourage all our clients to include it. Someone may have heard the story of a particular item before, but you stand a much greater chance of the item being kept and appreciated if you record it again in writing.

Whenever I (Josh) think of gifts and memories lists, I think of my grandmother, who lived to be 104 years old. She loved clocks. Over the years, she'd collected a house full of them, and she wanted to leave one to each of her children and grandchildren. To help her remember who was going to receive each clock, she placed sticky notes with people's names on the bottom of every clock. As she got older, she would change her mind about which people she wanted to receive which clock. And whenever she changed her mind, she would move all the sticky notes around. A simple gifts and memories list would have made the process a lot easier for her, but the mental picture of her swapping all those notes still brings a smile to my face.

The gifts and memories list is the legal version of my grandmother's sticky notes, and it's just as easy to change. Simply destroy the old one, write a new one, and sign it.

GIFTS AND MEMORIES LISTS AND THE GOALS OF RELATIONAL ESTATE PLANNING

The gifts and memories list is a great tool for relational estate planning. It helps you both preserve memories and leave a legacy.

GOAL 3: A GIFTS AND MEMORIES LIST LEAVES A LEGACY BY PASSING ON ITEMS AND STORIES THAT REMIND OTHERS OF YOU

Often, the things that are most meaningful to people have little to no monetary value. Of course, it's very important to leave your most valuable assets to the right beneficiary. But years down the road, when the money has been spent and the property has been sold, those things won't be what make your family and friends think of you and smile.

It'll be the ring that was your 16th birthday present, the handmade wooden trunk you built, the cookbook of favorite recipes scrawled in your handwriting, or the antique china that used to make parties and get-togethers feel special. These kinds of possessions represent a life and a person more than money ever could. The gifts and memories list allows you to pass on these items as part of your legacy.

GOAL 4: GIFTS AND MEMORIES LISTS PRESERVE MEMORIES BY LEAVING MEMORABLE ITEMS TO LOVED ONES

Has your nephew always loved sitting in your recliner when he comes to visit? Do you have old journals you know your little sister would love to read? Would your best friend want the knick-knacks you've collected from your weekend excursions together through the years? By giving personal items that were important to you to your loved ones, you can help preserve the memories they represent.

And it's not just limited to shared memories. You can use the gift and memories list to pass on heirlooms or treasured possessions that are part of your story or your family's history. We recently met a gentleman whose prized possession was a musket his ancestor had carried in the Civil War. He used a gifts and memories list not only to leave it to his son but also to record the story of that ancestor and how it had been passed down through the family.

If you are not sure who you want to receive a certain item or items, that's fine. Feel free to start your gifts and memories list with just a few items. You can easily change and add to it in the future. Starting a list might give you some perspective on what you want to be passed on after your death and what you'd rather give away while you're still living.

PRACTICAL TIPS FOR USING A GIFTS AND MEMORIES LIST IN RELATIONAL ESTATE PLANNING

TIP 1: THINK CREATIVELY ABOUT THE ITEMS YOU COULD LEAVE TO PRESERVE SPECIAL MEMORIES.

As we discussed in the Section One, leaving someone a physical item is a great way to preserve memories, which have the power to comfort your loved ones, even while they grieve for you. Thus, our first tip is to take the time to think about what you could leave to someone that will preserve a memory. It doesn't have to be big to be meaningful. But it will require some creativity and thought on your part to have the largest impact.

TIP 2: INCLUDE MEMORIES AND STORIES ON THE GIFT AND MEMORIES LIST.

If you only use a gifts and memories list to list out the items you want to give and the people receiving them, you'll miss a huge opportunity to preserve memories in writing. Many times, the person receiving an item forgets why it was important or where it came from.

This almost happened to me (Josh) with my great uncle's medals. In my room when I was growing up, there was a case of World War II Army medals. I knew it had come from my grandmother's family, but I had no idea whose medals they were. When I moved out, I intended to leave the case behind because it didn't mean anything to me. Fortunately, my father mentioned that they were my great uncle's medals. He had died when I was five and wanted me to have them. Now, all of a sudden, the case meant something, and I consider it a treasured possession. But without that story, I would have stored the case in a dusty attic and left it behind without a second thought. So make sure you take the time to explain why the items you are leaving are important to you.

TIP 3: GIVE THINGS AWAY NOW

And that brings us to our last thought concerning your personal possessions. Once you've made your list, consider giving away certain items now. This will make your family and friends' job easier when you are gone, plus you'll get the pleasure of watching your loved ones receive and enjoy the items. Evaluate for yourself when you are ready to give things away. There's no pressure, and there's no right or wrong way to do it.

The gifts and memories list is a wonderful tool that can help you pass on possessions in a manner that encourages, uplifts and strengthens those close to you.

CHAPTER 11 SUMMARY

A gifts and memories list is a tool you can use to leave specific items of personal property to specific individuals. For it to be enforceable in Virginia, it must be in writing, signed, and limited to personal property.

Gifts and memories lists can be used to accomplish Goals 3 and 4 of relational estate planning:

- Goal 3: Gifts and memories lists leave a legacy by allowing you to pass on items and stories that remind others of you.

- Goal 4: Gifts and memories lists preserve memories by leaving memorable items to loved ones.

Our three tips for gifts and memories lists are:

- Tip 1: Think creatively about which items you could leave to preserve memories.

- Tip 2: Include memories or stories on the gifts and memories list.

- Tip 3: Give things away now.

TOOL 7: PLANNED GIVING TO CHARITIES

"IF THERE BE ANY TRUER MEASURE OF A MAN THAN BY WHAT HE DOES, IT MUST BE BY WHAT HE GIVES."

-Robert South

As an estate, elder, and probate attorney, I (Josh) see death and the heartache that accompanies it every day. I watch the dying and their loved ones struggle with fear, physical and emotional pain, grief, depression, and more. But amid this darkness, I also see incredible light. I see love, strength, sacrifice, and hope. One way this light shines is when a dying person intentially leaves a legacy, something that says, "This is what my life meant, this is what I cared about, this is what I thought was important." Such self-sacrifice in the face of death is an incredible gift to everyone who sees it. There are many ways to communicate a legacy, but one powerful way is through planned giving.

The phrase "planned giving" means giving to a cause or a charity in a thoughtful, organized manner or creating a plan to give in the future. It's an avenue by which you can minimize taxes and, more importantly, give to others after you and your family have been provided for.

The best way to give depends on your circumstances. For many of our clients, planned giving simply means leaving a percentage of their estate to a charity when they pass. For others, it means setting up a stream of income for a loved one while they are alive and then providing for the assets to be distributed to a charity after they are gone. For someone else, it may mean setting up a charitable trust to take advantage of a tax deduction now for a gift that will be made later. Let's take a deeper look at the three main methods of planned giving.

GIFTS AT DEATH

The most common method of planned giving is setting up a gift to be given at the time of your passing. You can do this with either a will, a trust, or a beneficiary designation on a retirement or investment account or life insurance.

To give to a charity in your will or trust, you simply include that charity as one of the beneficiaries. You can either leave them a specific monetary amount or a percentage of your entire estate. For a retirement account, investment account, or life insurance, you will need to change the beneficiary designation on that account or policy to list the charity.

Our local hospice, Blue Ridge Hospice, is a wonderful organization that shares many of our relational estate planning values. Over the years, we have helped quite a few clients update their estate plans to leave some portion of their estate to Blue Ridge Hospice. One gentleman we knew received hospice services for several months before his death. He was so impressed with the care he received, that he told everyone who stopped by to see him about it. But, he wanted to do more. So, he changed the beneficiary of his 401k to be Blue Ridge Hospice. He told us he wanted to make sure that Blue Ridge Hospice could continue serving our community after he was gone. This is a great example of using planned giving to create a legacy.

CHARITABLE TRUSTS AND ANNUITIES

There are also several types of trusts that you can use as part of charitable giving. These trusts are unique because they allow you to receive an immediate tax deduction for gifts in the future.

CHARITABLE REMAINDER TRUST

A charitable remainder trust allows you to keep or give to a beneficiary the income from a certain asset or assets for a period of time or for the life of the beneficiary. When that period is up, whatever is left of the assets is given to your designated charity. This allows you to create a stream of income for yourself or others until it's no longer needed.

We recently worked with a couple, Dan and Sue, who had one son, Jimmie. Unfortunately, Jimmie had made some very poor financial decisions. He had filed bankruptcy twice and believed that money should be spent before it could be lost. Dan and Sue had carefully saved their whole lives and amassed quite a bit of assets. They knew that Jimmie would spend it all very quickly if they left him the money outright. Instead, they created a charitable remainder trust that will pay Jimmie a set amount each month. After they are gone and after Jimmie dies, any leftover money will be paid to their local SPCA.

CHARITABLE LEAD TRUST

A charitable lead trust is a trust in which you give the income from certain assets to a charity for a time. When the designated time is up, the assets are given back to you or to your loved ones. This trust allows you to support a charity, obtain a tax deduction, and keep caring for yourself or family.

CHARITABLE ANNUITY

A charitable annuity is a contract you enter into with a charity wherein you pay them a lump sum, and they agree to make payments to you or someone else for a period of time. This is another method by which you can create a stream of income for yourself or something else while also supporting a charity and receiving a tax deduction.

GIFTS OF APPRECIATED INVESTMENTS

The final method of planned giving is to give appreciated investments. These are investments that have increased in value, and if you sold them, you would owe capital gains taxes. By gifting these assets (instead of cash), you can give more than you would otherwise be able to because the charity does not have to pay capital gains tax. For all of these options, we recommend that you speak with a tax professional to ensure you receive the maximum tax savings from such gifts.

PLANNED GIVING AND RELATIONAL ESTATE PLANNING

Unlike the other tools we have considered, planned giving is focused on just one goal of relational estate planning: leaving a legacy.

GOAL 3: PLANNED GIVING LEAVES A LEGACY BY SUPPORTING CAUSES THAT WERE IMPORTANT TO YOU.

Planned giving is a great way to highlight and emphasize your legacy. Money speaks, and by donating money to a cause or organization when you pass, you will be reminding your family, friends, and community of what was important to you. You will also be supporting that organization so it can accomplish its mission.

Of course, some of these benefits can be gained just by giving. Planned giving, however, allows you to give more, reduce taxes, worry less, and make a long-term impact.

GIVE MORE

By giving taxable assets to a charity, you can give a much larger gift than you could give anyone else. This is because gifts to charities are tax-deductible. So, if you were to give a portion of your 401k or IRA to a family member, they would have to pay income and estate taxes on it. Depending on the specific circumstances, this can be as much as 77% of the total gift in Virginia, and more in other states. In other words, a gift of $100,000.00 would only be worth $23,000.00 to the recipient. However, if you were to make that same gift to a charity or non-profit, it would receive and be able to use the entire $100,000.00.

GIVE TO REDUCE TAXES

Planned giving, if done right, can allow you to reduce your current and future income taxes, estate taxes, and capital gains taxes. For example, you could create a charitable trust which provides you or your beneficiaries with an immediate income tax deduction but still allows you to use some of the funds you put in it.

GIVE WITHOUT WORRY

Planned giving also allows you to give after you have made sure you and your family have been provided for. You can either delay giving until certain needs are met or give in a way that allows you to retain use of funds until they are no longer needed. This means you can make a difference while at the same time protecting your loved ones.

GIVE TO MAKE A LONG-TERM IMPACT

Many organizations use planned gifts for major projects or improvements. By giving in this manner, you can help complete such a project or expand a charity's reach. And you get the reward of knowing your gift will be multiplied and have a meaningful, long-lasting impact.

PRACTICAL TIPS FOR PLANNED GIVING

TIP 1: MAKE SURE YOU CHOOSE YOUR CHARITIES CAREFULLY.

Not all organizations and charities are equally effective or even credible. Make sure you take the time to investigate the charity or organization to whom you are leaving money. They need to share your values and be a good steward of your legacy.

TIP 2: CONSIDER MAKING YOUR PLANNED GIVING CONDITIONAL ON THE SIZE OF YOUR ESTATE.

For many of our clients, their first and most important goal is to protect and provide for their loved ones. If that is your concern, then you may wish to consider setting up your plan so the gift only occurs if the total value of your estate is more than a certain amount. In this way, you can make your loved ones are cared for first.

TIP 3: CONSIDER ALL THE TAX IMPLICATIONS FROM GIVING.

Make sure to consider how to maximize the amount of your tax savings. For most of our clients, one way to ensure tax savings is to make sure all the gifts come from tax-deferred funds. If this an option you want to explore, make sure you consult with a tax professional before you make any official plans.

Planned giving is a rewarding and visible way to leave your legacy, and we believe it can be done without compromising your other relational goals. In fact, it can serve as a wonderful reminder of your values and an example for them to follow.

CHAPTER 12 SUMMARY

Planned giving is giving to a cause or a charity in a thoughtful, organized manner that is designed to maximize your impact, minimize taxes, and give to others after you and your family have been provided for. Planned giving can include gifts at death, charitable trusts and annuities, and gifts of appreciated assets.

Planned giving accomplishes Goal 3 of relational estate planning. It allows you to leave a legacy by supporting causes that were important to you.

Our three tips for planned giving are:

- Tip 1: Make sure to choose your charities carefully.

- Tip 2: Consider making your planned giving conditional on the size of your estate.

- Tip 3: Consider all the tax implications from giving.

CHAPTER 13:

FUNERAL ARRANGEMENTS AND DIRECTIVE

"THERE IS LOVE IN HOLDING AND THERE IS LOVE IN LETTING GO."

- Elizabeth Berg

The last tool in the arsenal of relational estate planning is funeral arrangements or directives. Funeral arrangements are a non-legal, non-binding set of instructions you put together about your wishes for your funeral and burial. You can put it in your estate guide and inventory or in a separate letter for your family or friends.

However, if you want to ensure your instructions are followed, you should use a funeral directive. A funeral directive is a legal document that allows you to appoint an agent to make funeral and burial decisions. It can also include directions for how you want to be buried, what you'd like to happen at your funeral, and how you want it paid for.

FUNERAL ARRANGMENTS AND DIRECTIVES AND RELATIONAL ESTATE PLANNING

Funeral arrangements and directives allow you to avoid conflict, highlight your legacy, and ease burdens for your loved ones.

GOAL 2: FUNERAL DIRECTIVES AVOID CONFLICT ABOUT YOUR FUNERAL AND BURIAL

Despite my (Anna) frugal, no-nonsense grandmother's attitude of "just put my body in the plainest wood box you can find and stick me in the ground," official burial and funeral arrangements aren't that simple. They can get way more involved, complicated, and expensive than you might believe.

Although loved ones fighting about funerals is not as common as them fighting about money, it still happens often. A funeral directive avoids this conflict by specifying what you want for your funeral and burial and appointing an agent who has the legal authority to carry out your wishes. Under Virginia law, your closest relatives get to make the decision about your funeral and burial, unless you have a funeral directive that gives one person authority to act. If you think that conflict between your loved ones is a possibility, then you should use a funeral directive, not just make funeral arrangements.

Several years ago, we had a client from Kenya. Her biggest concern was that if she died, her family would insist on flying her back to Kenya and spend all of her assets on a huge funeral there. However, she wanted to leave a legacy by giving what she had to several environmental non-profits she believed in. So, she created a funeral directive that required a green, environmentally friendly funeral and burial here in the United States. This funeral directive not only supported her legacy by requiring a simple and green funeral and burial, but it also preserved her funds for use by the environmental non-profits she supported.

GOAL 3: FUNERAL ARRANGEMENTS AND DIRECTIVES HIGHLIGHT YOUR LEGACY IN YOUR FUNERAL

Your funeral is a wonderful opportunity to impact not only your family and friends but also other members of your community. What do you want people to remember about you? What do you want them to focus on? What aspects of your life should be highlighted? What causes should be supported? The best funerals are not dark and gloomy affairs, but moving and memorable celebrations. By making funeral arrangements or creating a funeral directive, you can make sure your funeral and burial communicate your legacy.

GOAL 5: FUNERAL ARRANGEMENTS AND DIRECTIVES EASE BURDENS BY REDUCING THE NUMBER OF DECISIONS THAT HAVE TO BE MADE AFTER YOU ARE GONE

When you pass away, the people closest to you will be experiencing their own mixture of emotions, memories, and grief. That is the nature of loss, and though you can't prevent the heartache they may feel, you can make their lives easier and less complicated by arranging the details of your funeral and burial ahead of time.

PRACTICAL TIPS FOR USING FUNERAL ARRANGEMENTS AND DIRECTIVES

TIP 1: PRE-ARRANGE YOUR FUNERAL, BUT DON'T PREPAY IT.

People usually have these two questions as they plan for their funeral and burial: What details do I need to pre-arrange? What fees do I need to prepay? This is our rule of thumb: pre-arrange your funeral and burial, but don't prepay them. A prepaid funeral is risky. Many funeral plans can't be changed once paid for, and you don't know for sure that the funeral home you choose will still be in business when you die.

Of course, this is just a general rule, and there are exceptions.

For example, many people purchase a family burial plot to ensure that they all can be buried together. There are other fees you may wish to prepay, but be careful not to lock yourself into things that could potentially change.

TIP 2: USE A MEMORIAL SOCIETY TO COMPARE RATES AND SERVICES FOR FUNERALS AND BURIALS

There are many options for funerals and burials, and costs, even for the same service, often vary between funeral homes. We recommend you educate yourself and compare prices before making any decisions. One great resource for learning about your options is a Memorial Society. A Memorial Society is a non-profit organization that provides free information about the services offered by funeral homes and cemeteries in an area and how much they cost.

TIP 3: LEAVE DETAILED INSTRUCTIONS FOR YOUR FUNERAL AND BURIAL

Write down your funeral and burial plan in detail. You can't expect your loved ones to remember what you said at one time or another. Make it easy for them. Write it down and make sure several people know where the instructions are. If you are using a funeral directive, make sure the plan is in the directive, that the directive mentions the plan, and that you tell your family where to find it.

TIP 4: HAVE FUNDS EASILY ACCESSIBLE FOR YOUR FUNERAL AND BURIAL

As we mentioned above, you should avoid paying for your funeral or burial in advance. However, your funeral and burial will eventually need to be paid for, and one way to ease burdens for your loved ones is to make sure they have enough money available to them.

Because funerals often have to happen quickly or unexpectedly, your loved ones may not be able to access your money through the normal processes. We recommend you have another method available to them, such as a payable on death account or a special life insurance policy called burial insurance. Having money that is easily accessible will allow your loved ones to pay for your funeral and burial without a hassle.

CHAPTER 13 SUMMARY

Funeral arrangements are non-legal instructions expressing your wishes for your funeral and burial. A funeral directive is a legal document that allows you to appoint an agent to make funeral and burial decisions. If you are confident there will not be conflict over your funeral and burial, you can add simple funeral arrangemets to your estate guide and inventory. However, if conflict over your choices is a possibility, you should use a funeral directive.

Funeral arrangements and directives can be used to meet Goals 2, 3, and 5 of relational estate planning:

- Goal 2: Funeral directives avoid conflict about your funeral and burial.

- Goal 3: Funeral arrangements and directives allow you to highlight your legacy in your funeral.

- Goal 5: Funeral arrangements and directives ease burdens by reducing the number of decisions to be made when you are gone.

Our tips for funeral arrangements and directives are:

- Tip 1: Pre-arrange your funeral, but don't prepay it.

- Tip 2: Use a memorial society to compare rates and services for funerals and burials.

- Tip 3: Leave detailed instructions for your funeral and burial.

- Tip 4: Have funds easily accessible to pay for your funeral and burial.

SECTION TWO SUMMARY: TOOLS OF RELATIONAL ESTATE PLANNING

These are the eight tools of relational estate planning:

- Tool 1: Last Will and Testament
- Tool 2: Ethical Will
- Tool 3: Estate Guide and Inventory
- Tool 4: Trust
- Tool 5: Beneficiary Designation
- Tool 6: Gifts and Memories List
- Tool 7: Planned Giving
- Tool 8: Funeral Arrangements and Directive.

As we mentioned before, every relational estate plan should include the first three tools. Whether your plan needs any of the other five tools will depend on your goals and your loved ones.

At this point, we hope you are forming a vision for what a relational estate plan can accomplish for you and your loved ones, and that you have an idea of which tools you will need to implement your plan. Section Three provides you with next steps, guides and resources practical advice, details, and resources to help you get started with your Relational Estate Plan.

NEXT STEPS AND RESOURCES

"YOU WANT TO BE GOOD FOR THE ONES YOU LOVE, BECAUSE YOU
KNOW THAT YOUR TIME WITH THEM WILL END UP BEING TOO SHORT,
NO MATTER HOW LONG IT IS."

-Stephen King

We know that relational estate planning can seem like a lofty and out-of-reach philosophy. How do you turn all these ideas and options into concrete steps you can implement? Section Three is designed to help you do just that. In the next few chapters, we will equip you to translate the relational estate planning principles to your individual life.

The first chapter contains next steps you can to take to create your own relational estate plan. The second chapter addresses the unique situations that parents or grandparents of children under 18 face and offers advice for how to approach them with a relational estate plan. The third chapter is designed to help business owners create a relational estate plan that includes their business. The fourth chapter contains an overview of the tax laws that impact estate planning. The fifth chapter contains a guide to Virginia's estate planning laws. The sixth chapter contains a glossary of estate planning terms for you to reference as you learn more about the estate planning world and begin working with an attorney. The last chapter includes links to more estate planning resources we have published online.

CHAPTER 14:

_____

HOW TO CREATE YOUR OWN

RELATIONAL ESTATE PLAN

_____

"SOME PEOPLE CAN'T WRAP THEIR HEADS AROUND DEATH. AND
THESE PEOPLE LEAVE A MESS AFTER THEM. DID THEY THINK THEY WERE
IMMORTAL?"

-*Margareta Magnusson, "The Gentle Art of Swedish Death Cleaning"*

We've covered a lot of ground in these pages, but the task of creating your own relational estate plan may still seem overwhelming. Here are a few concrete steps to get you started.

STEP 1: IDENTIFY YOUR KEY RELATIONSHIPS AND MAKE A LIST OF YOUR ASSETS.

Your relational estate plan starts with your relationships and ends with your assets. Your first step should be to make sure you have a list of each. If you have minor children in your life or own a business, make sure you read through the guides in the next few chapters that deal with each of these unique situations.

STEP 2: PERSONALIZE THE FIVE RELATIONAL ESTATE PLANNING GOALS.

After you make a list of your relationships and assets, you need to personalize the relational estate planning goals. How will they work in your life and with your family, friends and community? Hopefully, you have already been thinking about this as you read through this book. But, if you need some help, we have a free guide you can use. You can download it using the link in the resources chapter.

STEP 3: SELECT AND START CREATING THE NON-LEGAL TOOLS IN YOUR PLAN.

As you may recall, several of the tools (the ethical will, estate guide and inventory, gifts and memories list, and funeral arrangements) are not legal documents. This means you can safely draft these without help from an attorney. Your next step should be decide which of these tools you will need in your plan and to start creating them. Remember, everyone should have an ethical will and estate guide and inventory. If you need help in creating these tools, we have included links to guides and forms in our resources chapter.

STEP 4: CONTACT AN EXPERIENCED ESTATE PLANNING ATTORNEY.

While you can do a lot on your own, we strongly recommend you work with an attorney to create the legal documents for your relational estate plan. You should try to find an attorney who practices in your state, who has experience with estate planning, and, most importantly, who is willing to help you create a relational estate plan focused on your goals.

PROVIDING FOR

MINOR CHILDREN

"ONE THING ABOUT HAVING A BABY IS THAT EACH STEP OF THE WAY
YOU SIMPLY CANNOT IMAGINE LOVING HIM ANY MORE THAN YOU
ALREADY DO, BECAUSE YOU ARE BURSTING WITH LOVE, LOVING AS
MUCH AS YOU ARE HUMANLY CAPABLE OF-AND THEN YOU DO, YOU
LOVE HIM EVEN MORE."

–Anne Lamott, Operating Instructions: A Journal of My Son's First Year

If you're a parent, we'd guess that your relational estate planning goals center largely around your children, regardless of their age. But if you have young children, then concern for them is probably an even bigger aspect of your plan. Where will they live if something happens to you? Who will raise them? How will they pay for college? These and similar questions might be humming at the forefront of your mind.

We get it. Our love for our children changes everything about the way we view life, and this love drives us to stop at nothing to protect, nurture, and keep them safe. Unfortunately, we live in a world where kids are not always healthy and cared for, where bad things happen to good families, and where legitimate threats to our children do exist. You need a relational estate plan to ensure your children are protected and provided for if you aren't around to do it yourself. To protect and provide for your young child or children, we suggest you take four steps in addition to using the other relational estate planning tools we have already discussed:

STEP 1: NAME A GUARDIAN TO LOVE AND CARE FOR YOUR MINOR CHILD

A guardian is a substitute parent. In Virginia and many other states, all parents have the legal right to name a guardian for their children if something happens to both of them. This person will have the right to legal custody of your child should something happen to both biological parents.

If you haven't named a guardian, the state will decide where the children go in the short term until a judge can review the case and make the final decision. Your child may be placed in an orphanage or with foster parents, or they may end up with relatives or friends you wouldn't want raising them. While we all would agree that it's important for the state to have a system to take care of orphans, most people don't want their children living with strangers or in a group home during such a traumatic time.

In Virginia, the guardian must be named in your will. If you correctly name a guardian, Virginia law requires that the person you've named be given immediate and permanent custody of your child should something happens to you.

The last thing your child needs is to be separated from people they know and love if they suffer the trauma of losing both parents. Sadly, they'll have enough to process and work through without being moved from home to home. So when you name a guardian for them, you guarantee your child will be cared for by the right people. In addition to naming one person as the primary guardian, we recommend you include one or more backups in your will in the event that your first choice is unable to step into their role at the time.

STEP 2: CREATE A MINOR'S TRUST TO PROTECT YOUR CHILD'S FINANCIAL FUTURE

By law, children are not in control of their own funds or

property until the age of 18. In Virginia, if you die before your child reaches that age, their assets will be managed under court supervision until their 18th birthday, at which time they will be given complete control of everything. We talked about this in the chapter on trusts, but think about it again. What child, at 18, should control large amounts of money? Your child might be incredibly responsible, but if they received your life savings right out of high school, the temptations would be enormous. To avoid this and to protect your child's financial future, we recommend you add a minor's trust to your relational estate plan.

A minor's trust is a mini-trust inside your will or living trust that states that your child will not receive any money from your estate until they reach a certain age you choose. Until then, a trustee you select manages the money for the child's benefit. This trustee can sensibly distribute funds for things like your child's education, travel, medical bills, and other living expenses. This tyep of trust can ensure that your child is well taken care of, but without giving them access to their inheritance until they've had a chance to mature and learn how to handle finances responsibly.

STEP 3: DESIGNATE BENEFICIARIES TO PROTECT YOUR CHILD

As we discussed in chapter 10, assets like retirement funds, such as financial accounts and insurance policies, allow you to list beneficiaries on them. If you have a minor child listed as your beneficiary on any of these accounts, these funds will go to them at the age of 18 regardless of any minor's trust you may have set up in your will or trust.

Not only that, but these funds are often tax-deferred. This means that income taxes have not yet been paid on these accounts. The government has many rules and requirements for how these accounts must be handled, and if your child does not use them properly, they will incur additional taxes and penalties. The last thing you want is for your child to get a large chunk of money at a young age, make rash decisions with it, and then have the IRS after them, demanding taxes and penalties. To avoid the risk, we recommend that you designate your minor's trust as the beneficiary of all such accounts. That way, all the money from these accounts will go to be used for your child. Your child will receive the funds when they reach the age you select.

While we believe this is the best way to protect your minor children, there is a downside to this plan. If you put tax-deferred monies in a trust, the trust will most likely have to pay more in taxes than your children would have if they had received the funds directly. However, to most of our clients, this is an acceptable trade-off since it protects their children.

STEP 4: PURCHASE LIFE INSURANCE TO ENSURE YOUR CHILD'S FINANCIAL NEEDS ARE MET

Lastly, make sure that you have enough disability and life insurance so that your child is taken care of financially when you are disabled or gone. A good insurance agent can assist you in figuring out exactly how much insurance you need. But be careful. Some dishonest insurance agents will try to sell you more insurance than you need. We recommend that you meet with several different reputable financial advisers or insurance agents and compare what they tell you.

We know your children are your greatest treasure. We know that you, like most parents out there, would do anything to protect and provide for them. A lot of things in this life are uncertain; don't let your child's future be one of them.

CHAPTER 16:

_____

RELATIONAL ESTATE PLANNING FOR

BUSINESS OWNERS

_____

"LET US ALL BE THE LEADERS WE WISH WE HAD."

-Simon Sinek, Leaders Eat Last

If you own a business, you're used to having decisions fall on your shoulders. So you won't be surprised to hear that there are quite a few different ways to plan for your business at the end of your life, and it can get complicated. But the relational goals remain the same. How can you use your business to protect and provide for your loved ones and leave a legacy while easing burdens? A business can be a tremendous legacy, but it can also be a tremendous headache for your loved ones if you don't plan properly. We aren't going to get into all the details of how to create an estate plan for your business here because it varies greatly from business to business and from owner to owner. Instead, we'll give you three principles that we believe every business owner should use as they create an estate plan for their business.

ESTATE PLANNING FOR YOUR BUSINESS: THREE KEY PRINCIPLES

_____

These three principles might seem obvious, but there's more to them than you might think. Take a look:

PRINCIPLE 1: DECIDE WHAT YOU WANT TO HAPPEN TO YOUR BUSINESS AFTER YOUR DEATH.

If you could choose exactly what would happen to your business when you die, what would you envision? It sounds basic, but in our experience, most business owners haven't thought about this, or if they have, they haven't thought realistically about it.

- Would your business carry on or shut down?
- Would your family need to liquidate your business assets to support themselves?
- Is your business part of your legacy? What could passing that legacy on look like?
- Could your business be purchased by an outside buyer? Would you rather it be taken over by a current employee or family member?
- If your business continues, who will keep it running during the time of transition after your death?
- Will your business continue to function in the same way, or is it too owner-centric for that to be possible?

There are a hundred scenarios for what could happen to your business when you're gone, but questions like these will help you decide which direction to go. Keep the goals of relational estate planning in mind-protecting and providing for your loved ones, avoiding conflict, leaving a legacy, preserving memories, and easing burdens. Once you have an idea for how your business should look after you are gone, you can think about Principle 2:

PRINCIPLE 2: CREATE AN ESTATE PLAN FOR YOUR BUSINESS.

Again, this isn't rocket science. You need an estate plan for your business. But sometimes, this is easier said than done. Businesses, especially small businesses, run into their own unique set of issues with estate planning. The biggest of these problems is replacing the role of the owner in the business. Many small businesses like medical practices, law firms, or other professionals revolve heavily around one person practicing their trade, and without that person, the business doesn't exist. Even when there is more than one owner, all the owners are normally vital, if not irreplaceable, in the business. So unless you don't care what happens to your business when you are gone, you must create a realistic plan. This could be that the business shuts down in an orderly fashion, or that it is sold, or that someone else takes over and runs it. All of these scenarios require planning and for you to answer specific questions, such as:

- Who will do your job the day, the month, and the year after you are gone?
- What will they need to know?
- How will they be paid?
- Will the business be sold?
- How will it be run in the meantime?
- Who will buy the business?

Your plan must address all of these questions, and then you'll need the right person or people to implement the plan. This leads us to the final principle.

PRINCIPLE 3: CREATE A TEAM OF PEOPLE TO IMPLEMENT YOUR BUSINESS ESTATE PLAN.

Our friend, Jim, is a business owner with three children. Two are heavily involved in the business, and one isn't. When Jim began thinking about how he could protect and provide for his children, he recognized that the business and his two children who worked for it needed each other. It makes sense to leave the business to them because it was a huge part of their lives. But he also wanted to be fair to his other child. So he set up his estate plan to leave the business to the two children who worked for it and used life insurance to create an inheritance for his third child.

Jim also recognized that his two children in the business were not ready yet to run it by themselves. He loved them, but he knew they couldn't replace him. So he arranged for other key employees to remain at the business after he passed to help his children run the business. He also made sure the two children in the business know his key advisors-his attorney, accountant, and financial advisor. He put a lot of thought into how everything will work when he is gone, and he was and remains convinced of something we advocate continually: A team of people who know what's going on with your business and are ready to step in at your death is key to a successful business estate plan.

If you have employees, some of them will almost certainly be a part of this team. But we also suggest that you have an ongoing relationship with an attorney, accountant, and one or more business advisors, just like Jim did. All of these people should have a basic knowledge of your business estate plan and their role in it. With a good team to help with the transition, your business can be a tremendous asset to your relational goals.

THE BEST BUSINESS ESTATE PLANS

Every year, we see businesses come to messy ends after an owner has died. It shouldn't be that way. You've worked too hard on your business to have it implode after you are gone. We believe it is possible for every business owner to set up their business to be a blessing and not a burden to their family and employees, even after they're gone. But it will require a well-thought-out plan and a great team. If you follow the principles in this chapter and seek help from relevant experts, you can ensure your business provides for your loved ones and leaves a legacy of what you have built.

IT'S TIME TO TALK TAXES

Most of us have played Monopoly. If you've been lucky enough to pick up the Community Chest card that says, "You Inherit $100," you've seen this classic illustration: Uncle Milburn Pennybags (renamed "Mr. Monopoly" in 1999) clasps his hands around his bald head and gapes at the crowd of salesmen handing him brochures advertising "Rolls Royce," "World Tour," and "Buy a Yacht." What should he spend his cash on first?! But, stop! Wait a minute. If you're thinking of blessing someone with a big old inheritance check, you've got to consider something we haven't talked much about yet: taxes, taxes, taxes.

THREE TYPES OF TAXES

If you're going to accomplish your relational estate planning goals, it's best to keep as many of your assets within your control as possible, unless one of your goals is to voluntarily fund the federal government.

Knowing what taxes your heirs may have to pay, and setting things up so they have to pay as little as possible is also a big way to ease their burdens after you die. The fewer government requirements your loved ones have to worry about, the better.

The world of taxes can be technical and complicated, but we will try to make things as simple as we can. There are three main types of taxes that affect estate planning: estate taxes, income taxes, and capital gains taxes.

ESTATE TAXES

At this point, only the very wealthy in the U.S. are affected by estate taxes. But that's not always been the case, and it could change at any point, so you should understand the concept.

At the end of your life, the government will look at what you've given away during your lifetime, as well as what you're gifting to your heirs. If those two categories combined equal more than about $11,000,000.00 for a single person, or about $22,000,000.00 for a couple (the actual amounts are a bit higher), a tax of around 40% will be applied to everything you own over those amounts. The actual amounts and percentages vary slightly depending on the situation, but the amounts we have given are a good rule of thumb. If you think estate taxes could apply to you, you'll want to consult an expert about how to reduce the amount your heirs will owe. Also, if you do owe estate taxes, you will need to make sure you don't run afoul of the related generation-skipping tax.

INCOME TAXES

Unlike estate taxes, which tax what you give, income taxes tax what you earn. You are probably much more familiar with these taxes than you want to be. As with a living person, an estate can earn money if it owns investments or a business. But more frequently, estates owe income taxes because they contain tax-deferred funds such as retirement accounts.

Income invested in certain retirement accounts (like a 401k or a traditional IRA) is untaxed, so when it's time to pull that money out and use it, you (or your estate or beneficiary) must pay income taxes on it.

This kind of money is referred to as tax-deferred funds. People who inherit tax-deferred funds have various options about how and when they have to pay the taxes owed on those funds. What you need to know is that how the funds are inherited determines how many options someone has. If you want your loved ones to have the greatest flexibility to reduce the income taxes owed on tax-deferred funds, you need to craft a plan that addresses them.

Your estate or trust also has the potential to continue earning income after you die. This could be income from interest earned on a savings account, the sale of certain investments, or profit from a business. And income always means taxes, whether you're dead or alive. Unfortunately, an estate or trust is taxed at the highest tax rate much more quickly than an individual. For example, right now, an individual will only pay the highest income tax rate (currently 37%) if they earn $500,000 or more annually. However, a trust or estate will pay the highest income tax rate if it earns $12,750 or more. The easiest way to avoid these increased income taxes is to set your estate plan up to distribute your assets quickly after your death. There are other options to avoid these taxes as well, but you should consult with an expert to make sure you get this set up properly.

CAPITAL GAINS TAXES

Capital gains taxes are taxes on money you gain through investments. If you buy stock in Starbucks for $50.00 and later sell it for $100.00, the government will tax you on that $50.00 increase. Now, capital gains taxes at the time of your death are impacted by a rule called a "step-up in basis." Step-up in basis is a great rule; it simply means that whoever inherits your assets will only owe capital gains on the increase in value after you died. Any amounts the investments increased in value before you died are not taxed!

For example, go back to your Starbucks stock. You bought it for $50.00, and let's say you pass away without selling it. If it's worth $150.00 when you die, that's its new basis under the step-up in basis rule. Now let's say that your daughter inherits the stock, hangs on to it for a year, then sells it for $175.00. Instead of having to pay taxes on the difference between the original $50.00 and $175.00 (which is what you would have had to pay if you still owned it), she'll only have to pay taxes on the difference between $150.00 and $175.00. She gets a substantial tax break.

For this reason, you want to think carefully before selling or giving away investments that have appreciated in value if there is a chance you can pass them on to your heirs.

Like we said at the beginning of this chapter, taxes can get complicated. They can also get expensive. Mark Twain once said, "The only difference between a tax man and a taxidermist is that the taxidermist leaves the skin." It's funny, but it's also not funny. While it's not enjoyable to think about taxes, everyone should take the time to understand the basics and ensure that their hard-earned money is used to achieve their goals, not to pay more than necessary.

We have given you an aerial view of tax principles that can help you. But it can get complicated depending upon your financial situation. That's why we strongly recommend you consult with an estate planning attorney to get specific advice about how to reduce the amount of taxes you will owe.

ESTATE PLANNING IN VIRGINIA

Every state's requirements for wills, trusts, and estate distribution is a little different. This means if you made an estate plan years ago in Georgia, it might not meet all state requirements if you've moved to retire in North Carolina. But it's important for you to know how the state you're currently living in is going to affect your estate. So, what do Virginia residents need to know about their estate plans? Here are five main Virginia estate planning facts to keep in mind:

STANDARD SIGNATORY REQUIREMENTS

Similar to most other states, Virginia requires two witnesses at the signing of a will and encourages the use of a self-proving affidavit, notarized by a notary, to simplify the probate process for the will. These are common requirements in many states, and wills created in Virginia should be valid in most other states. Nevertheless, we always recommend our clients who move out of state speak with an estate planning attorney in their new state to ensure the documents will be effective there.

NO RESTRICTIONS ON OUT OF STATE GUARDIANS

Unlike several other states, Virginia does not prohibit or restrict naming a guardian for minor children if the guardian is not a Virginia resident. To put it differently, you can easily and without penalty name a guardian for your minor child or children, even if that individual lives in a different state.

RESTRICTIONS ON OUT OF STATE EXECUTORS

Unlike the guardian, Virginia does make things more difficult for out of state executors. If the resident of another state is named as an executor of a will, they'll have to (a) post a bond and (b) name a local agent for service of legal papers. Normally, the naming of an agent is not difficult or expensive, but getting a bond is always expensive and sometimes impossible if the named executor does not have good credit. As a result, Virginia residents should think carefully before naming someone who lives in a different state as their executor or backup executor.

NO SEPARATE ESTATE TAX

Virginia, unlike some other states, does not currently have an estate tax or an inheritance tax, which means going through the probate process is not as costly as it is in some other states.

SIMPLIFIED PROBATE OPTIONS

Virginia is more flexible than many other states when it comes to allowing simplified paths through probate.

Here are the instances when Virginia allows a simplified or summary probate:

- If the estate owns only real estate (land or anything permanently attached to land).
- If the estate owns less than $50,000.00 in personal property not including real estate.
- If the has the same person as both the executor and the sole beneficiary.

Virginia residents should keep all of these features in mind when putting together their relational estate plan.

VIRGINIA ESTATE PLANNING GLOSSARY

You will hear the following terms in the estate planning world, and we have included their definitions here for you reference. We have defined these terms according to how they are used in the state of Virginia.

Advance Medical Directive: A legally binding document that allows you to select the medical care and treatment you want to receive if you become incapacitated or unable to make decisions. It also allows you to designate a medical **agent** and empower them to make decisions for you if you become incapacitated or unable to make decisions.

Agent: A person you authorize to act in your place. They are also sometimes referred to as a **personal representative** or an attorney-in-fact.

Beneficiary: The person or organization you select [or designate] to receive property under your will, trust, or **beneficiary designation**.

Beneficiary Designation: An instruction to a bank or other financial institution to pay or transfer assets in an account to a certain person or organization when you die.

Bequeath: Technically, this means to give someone personal property in a will. It is frequently used more broadly to mean a gift of assets to a person or organization when you die.

Decedent: This is a person who has died. When used in regard to an **estate plan**, it normally refers the person who has died and whose assets are being distributed.

Devise: Technically, this means to give someone **real property** in a will. It is frequently used more broadly to mean a gift of assets to a person or organization when you die.

Estate Administration: The legal process by which a deceased person's debts are paid and their assets are distributed.

Estate Guide and Inventory: A non-legal document that allows you to give your **personal representative** a list of your assets and important instructions about your estate. It can include **funeral arrangements**, online account information, and contact information for professionals who can help your **personal representative.**

Estate Plan: In its strictest sense, an estate plan is a plan for how your assets (your estate) will be distributed when you die. However, it is often used in a broader sense to include your plan for your finances and care when you become incapacitated or are unable to make decisions. An estate plan is often made up of multiple parts, including:

- how you want to be cared for as you get older
- who gets to make decisions if you aren't able to make them
- how you want your assets used while you are alive
- funeral and burial arrangements
- what you want your legacy to be
- distribution and use of your assets when you are gone

It can include legal and non-legal documents and tools, such as wills, trusts, **financial powers of attorney, advance medical directives, ethical wills, estate guides and inventories, gifts and memories lists,** and **beneficiary designations.**

Estate Planning: The process of creating and updating an **Estate Plan.**

Ethical Will: A non-legal document designed to pass on your values, beliefs, experiences, and advice to your loved ones.

Financial Power of Attorney: A legally binding document in which you authorize someone else to make financial decisions for you. This person is referred to as your **agent.** A financial power of attorney is also sometimes referred to as a durable general power of attorney.

Funeral Arrangements: A non-legal set of instructions expressing your wishes about your funeral ceremony and burial. We encourage clients to put these in their **estate guide and inventory.**

Funeral Directive: A legal document authorizing a person of your choosing to make decisions about your funeral and burial.

Gifts and Memories List: A legal document that allows you to specify certain items of tangible personal property that you want given to certain people or organizations upon your death. It must be used with a will or a trust, and it can only be used for tangible personal property, not **real property** or money. It is also referred to as a personal property memorandum.

Grantor: Another term for the creator of a trust.

Guardian: A person named in a will or appointed by the court to care for a minor (under 18) child or a disabled adult.

Intestacy: A set of default rules about who will receive your assets if you die without a valid will. Each state has its own set of intestacy rules.

Last Will and Testament: A legally binding document that allows you to specify how you want your assets distributed after your death. The will is enforced through **probate.**

Personal Property Memorandum: Another name for a **gifts and memories list.**

Payable on Death Designation: A type of **beneficiary designation** that instructs a bank or financial institution to pay the funds in a certain account to a person or organization when you die.

Personal Representative: The person who will carry out your **estate plan** according to your will, if you have one, or the intestacy laws if you don't. In Virginia, this person is called an executor if you have a will and an administrator if you do not have a will or they are not named in your will.

Personal Property: All types of property (assets) that are not **real property.**

Planned Giving: A term for gifting money to a charitable organization in a thoughtful, organized manner, or creating a plan to bequeath money to that organization in the future.

Pour Over Will: A will that is created to work with a **living trust.** It normally dictates that all of your assets will be transferred to the living trust at your death.

Principal: A person who authorizes another to act on their behalf. You are the principal when you create a **financial power of attorney** or **advance medical directive.**

Probate: The process by which a court makes sure that the **personal**

representative follows the directions in your will, if you have one, or the **intestacy** laws if you do not.

Prudent Investor Rule: The default rule that your **personal representative** must invest all of your assets in a diversified portfolio of stocks instead of holding them as-is.

Real Property: All property that is either land or buildings attached to land.

Relational Estate Planning: A holistic **estate planning** philosophy that prioritizes your well-being and your relationships over your money and asset distribution.

Residue: The remainder of the assets in your estate after all expenses are paid and any specific gifts or bequests are made. Each will or trust should have a provision that states what will happen to the residue of your estate.

Right of Survivorship: A type of ownership that allows property that you own jointly with someone else to be automatically transferred to them when you die and vice versa.

Trust:

- **Trust, Charitable:** A trust designed to leave money to or benefit a charity.

- **Trust, Irrevocable:** A trust that may not be revoked by the creator after it is made.

- **Trust, Living:** a trust that is created and implemented while you are alive. It is normally created for the purpose of avoiding **probate** or protecting assets.

- **Trust, Minors:** A small trust included in a will or another trust which prevents a child or young adult from receiving their inheritance until they reach a certain age.

• **Trust, Revocable:** A trust that the creator has the right to change or revoke.

• **Trust, Special Needs:** a trust that is designed to provide for someone with a disability. It is normally created to ensure that the assets in the trust do not disqualify the disabled person from receiving government benefits, such as Medicaid.

• **Trust, Under-Age:** Another name for a **Minor's Trust**.

Trustee: The person or institution named by the creator of a trust to manage the trust property for the **beneficiaries** of the trust.

FURTHER RESOURCES

We've put together a list of resources to help you as you begin your relational estate planning journey. These resources will help you take the next steps in developing your own relational estate plan.

OUR BLOG

For more bite-sized discussions, tips, and advice on estate planning, check out our blog at www.relational.law/blog. We regularly publish short articles on many topics related to estate planning including new tips and techniques we have learned and changes in the law.

GUIDES AND WORKSHEETS

We have created a number of guides and worksheets specifically for the readers of this book. Here are a few you can find on our website.

- Relational Estate Planning Next Steps

- Ethical Will How-to Guide

- Ethical Will Form

- Estate Guide and Inventory Form

- Gifts and Memories List Form

Go to www.relational.law/fearless-book to access these guides and worksheets.

SUGGESTED READING

If you want to dive deeper into the goals and tools of Relational Estate Planning ®, here are a few of the books that we enjoyed and you may find helpful:

- *Ethical Wills: Putting Your Values On Paper* by Barry K. Baines, M.D.

- *Ethical Wills and How to Prepare Them: A Guide to Sharing Your Values from Generation to Generation* edited by Rabbi Jack Riemer and Dr. Nathaniel Stampfer

- *A Faithful Farewell: Living Your Last Chapter with Love* by Marilyn McEntyre

- *The Forever Letter: Writing What We Believe for Those We Love* by Elana Zaiman

- *The Gentle Art of Swedish Death Cleaning* by Margareta Magnusson

- *Splitting Heirs: Giving Your Money and Things to Your Children Without Ruining Their Lives* by Ron Blue with Jeremy White

EPILOGUE

In this book, we've attempted to paint a picture of how you can prepare differently for the end of your life. Death is a scary thing for most people, and in our society, we go to great lengths to avoid even thinking about it. But, regardless of our willingness to acknowledge it, our time is limited, and refusing to face that reality only leads to being unprepared.

What does it mean to die well? Contrary to popular belief, we don't think it has anything to do with someone dying at an old age, or with lots of money, or with having a list of grand achievements attached to one's name. We believe the best death is the one that is faced self-sacrificially. Men and women throughout history have shown us that the noblest deaths are those met with others in mind. Mothers and fathers have sacrificed themselves to save their children, soldiers have given their lives for their countrymen, people of immovable character have died to protect the defenseless. And while you might not be fighting a war or trying to save others from a catastrophe at the end of your life, a spirit of willing service can still drive you. Are you willing to focus on others instead of yourself? Are you willing to do everything you can to provide for them after you're gone? Dying with this kind of dignity requires a choice. It calls you to pursue a higher calling, that of putting others first during a time when it feels only natural to be focused on yourself.

Relational Estate Planning ® is one way to do this. We earnestly hope you will decide to own the parts of this philosophy that will work for you and those you hold dear. Not only will it be a gift to them, but it will also bring you comfort, freedom, and confidence. Approach your death generously, and gain the fearlessness that comes from ending well.

9 781734 553826